CARD GAMES
FOR FOUR

David Parlett

TEACH YOURSELF BOOKS
Hodder and Stoughton

First impression 1977

Copyright © 1977
David Parlett

ISBN 0 340 22232 8

Printed in Great Britain for
Hodder and Stoughton Paperbacks,
a division of Hodder and Stoughton Ltd,
Mill Road, Dunton Green, Sevenoaks, Kent
(Editorial Office, 47 Bedford Square, London WC1 3DP),
by Hazell Watson & Viney Ltd, Aylesbury, Bucks

To Roger and Penny Duce

CONTENTS

INTRODUCTION

All card games are divided into three sorts, of which one is called partnership, another solo, and the third cut-throat.

Four is a convenient number of players, as it gives a wide choice of games in all categories: two-against-two partnership games such as Whist, one-against-three games such as Solo, and all-against-all ('cut-throat') such as Rummy. All are represented in this collection, which is also designed to cater for all tastes by the primary selection of games on the basis of variety.

Some eyebrows may be raised at the exclusion of Contract Bridge. But for one thing there is already a whole *Teach Yourself* devoted to it, and for another I have included the unjustly neglected game of Contract Whist, which is virtually Bridge, but without the dummy. Anyone who learns Contract Whist will be able to sit down at the Bridge table and hold his own after a few minutes of further explanation. Whether he will find Bridge an improvement is an interesting question.

Taking the series title at its word, I have catered for complete beginners at cards by starting with the most elementary game and describing the basic mechanics of card-play in the simplest possible terms. The fact that Whist is also one of the deepest and most subtle of games does not detract from the ease with which it may be learnt – indeed, such qualifications only add to the value of the exercise. Start with Whist, and you can never go wrong.

For reference, technical terms are explained in a glossary on page 199.

Throughout the text I have used the abbreviation T to denote the Ten of a suit (A K Q J T 9 etc), for typographic convenience. I hope this will not give anyone an apoplexy.

My wife and usual band of wandering card-players have given much practical support to the cause of my researches, and I am grateful to them all. I acknowledge that the sample games of Partnership, Contract and Solo Whist are adapted from those presented in the standard works, while relieving all but myself of responsibility for any errors that may have slipped through.

NOTE TO THE TEXT

The winning card of any trick in the exposition of sample games is denoted by bold type:

A	B	C
♡**K**	♡2	♡5

e.g. A is the winner of the above hand.

Playing cards used in illustrations are reproduced by courtesy of Waddingtons Playing Card Co. Ltd.

PART I

PARTNERSHIP GAMES

I
WHIST
A game of tricks

Whist is not only one of the greatest games ever devised, but also mechanically the simplest and most archetypal of all card games. The absolute beginner at cards can pick it up in a few minutes, and, having played it a few times, will have gained enough experience in basic card-play to undertake any new card game, however complex, with complete confidence.

Whist, like Cribbage, is essentially an English game. At first it was played only by the unlettered and unsophisticated: in 1674, Charles Cotton forbore to detail it in his *Compleat Gamester*, on the ground that 'every child almost of eight years old hath a competent knowledge in that recreation'. Sixty years later the game was taken up by serious players, and in 1742 Edmond Hoyle published his first treatise on Whist, based on lecture notes compiled in his lucrative capacity as a private Whist-tutor to young gentleladies 'attended upon in their own home'. From it and from subsequent treatises on other games he made a fortune late in life and promptly bequeathed his name to posterity. The last and greatest authority was Dr Henry ('Cavendish') Jones, who in the latter decades of the nineteenth century expounded so brilliantly upon the 'scientific' and 'philosophical' principles of play as (some say) to drive it far beyond the reach of ordinary mortal intellect.

Cavendish may be accused of killing Whist through analysis, but the real culprit was the rising popularity of a closely related game called Bridge, of which modern Contract Bridge is a later development (see *Teach Yourself Contract Bridge*), and to which Whist is the ideal – indeed necessary – introduction. Whist is nowadays played in a less glorious manner as a somewhat old-fashioned family game and as an entertainment at social gatherings ('Whist drives'). Efforts being made to revive it, however, are well worthy of success, and no self-respecting card-player may consider his education complete without a solid grounding in this simple but subtle exercise in partnership play.

The following description is designed for complete (but not unintelligent) beginners at card play, and will serve as an introduction to basic mechanics and principles that underlie most of the other games in this book.

Preliminaries

Whist is a partnership game, the two players of each partnership sitting opposite each other. One member of each partnership should keep the score for both sides, as a double check on accuracy.

A rubber is the best of three games: if the same side wins the first two, a third is not played.

Each game is played 'five-up' – that is, the first side to reach or exceed a score of five points wins the game. As many rounds or deals are played as may be necessary for one side to make five.

Cards. The standard 52-card pack is used. It contains four suits of 13 cards each, designated spades (♠), hearts (♡), clubs (♣), diamonds (◇). The four suits are intrinsically equal in power and value, but at each deal one of them (at random) is promoted to the status of 'trump' suit, as explained later, and has power over the others.

The thirteen cards of each suit are called 'ranks', as they rank in power relatively to one another. Ace is the highest rank, followed by King, Queen and Jack, and Two is the lowest, the complete 'pecking order' being:

A K Q J T 9 8 7 6 5 4 3 2 (T = Ten)

Shuffle and deal. Decide who is to be the first dealer by any agreed means. The usual method is to spread the cards face down in a row, each player drawing one at random. Whoever draws the highest-ranking card (regardless of suit) deals first. (By tradition, Ace counts lowest, not highest, for this purpose.) If two players tie, they alone draw once more against each other.

The cards must be shuffled before each deal. Any one or more players may shuffle if they wish, but dealer has the right to shuffle last. He then deals the cards one by one face down around the table, starting with the player on his left and finishing with himself. Before adding the last card to his hand, however, he lays it face up on the table so that all can see it.

It should be noted that the deal and all play of the cards proceed clockwise around the table, as does the right to deal – i.e., the player on the left of the first dealer automatically becomes dealer in the second round, and so on.

Trumps. Dealer now adds the face-up (52nd) card to his own hand, announcing the suit of that card as the trump suit for this particular deal. This means that any card of the suit is superior to a card of any other suit in the pack, regardless of their rank. Thus the lowest trump, the Two, is higher than and may capture any non-trump Ace, and the Ace of trumps is the highest card in the pack. The non-trump suits are called plain suits or side suits.

Object. The object is for you and your partner to win more tricks between you than your opponents. The partnership winning the majority of tricks – seven or more – scores one point for every trick they take above six.

There may be an additional score for honours – the Ace, King, Queen and Jack of trumps. If by the end of the deal it becomes known that one partnership has held three or four trump honours between them, having been dealt them at the beginning, they score respectively two or four points. Each player should therefore mentally note before play whether he himself holds one or more of the honours cards.

Play. The usual rules of trick-taking apply. The player left of dealer leads to the first trick. You must follow suit to the card led if possible; if not, you may trump or discard. The trick is won by the highest card of the suit led, or by the highest trump if any are played. The winner of a trick leads to the next.

Explanation. The 'usual rules' outlined above appear constantly throughout this book and will be understood by all card-players. For beginners, however, they may be explained at greater length as follows.

A trick consists of four cards, one contributed by each player in turn. The person who plays the best card wins the trick.

The player at dealer's left starts by playing any card face up to the middle of the table. In clockwise rotation the other players each contribute a card face up, but are obliged to play a card of the *same suit* as the first one if they can. This is called 'following suit to the card led'. If everyone follows suit, the player of the highest-ranking card wins the trick, which he signifies by gathering up the four cards and laying them face down on the table before him in a neat, squared-up pile. (Tricks won by the same player should be kept separate from one another to facilitate counting, but overlapping one another to save space. As Charles Cotton (in the *Compleats Gamester*) puts it, 'Lay your tricks angle-wise, that you may the more facilely compute them'). Whoever wins the trick then leads a card to start the second trick, and so on until all thirteen have been played and won, the winner of each automatically leading to the next.

If a player is unable to follow to a card led from a plain suit, he may seek to win the trick by playing a trump, and if he is the only person to do so he wins the trick. This is known as 'ruffing'. The others must still follow to the suit led if possible, but again anyone who cannot may play a trump. If more than one trump is played to a trick, it is won by the player of the highest-ranking trump.

Anyone who cannot follow suit is not obliged to trump but may, if he prefers, play from another plain suit. This is called 'discarding', which can never win the trick.

A player may choose to discard, as, for example, when his partner has already won the trick so he himself has no need to contest it, or he may be forced to, as when he holds no cards of the suit led and no trumps either.

It follows that if a trump is led, a player who is void in (has none of) that suit will be forced to discard, and cannot contest it.

Revoking. The penalty for a revoke is three points. (A player revokes when he fails to follow suit even though able to do so. If the revoke can be corrected in time there is no penalty, but usually it does not become known until later in the play. If a player can be shown to have revoked, the opposing side may either score three points for itself or deduct three points from its opponents.)

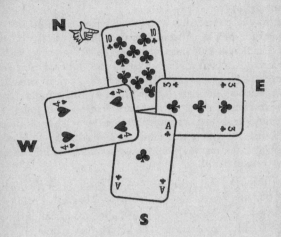

FIGURE I

How tricks are played, illustrating 'the usual rules of trick-taking'. Hearts are trumps. North, to start, decides to open a round of clubs and leads the Ten. East, obliged to follow suit but unable to beat the Ten, discards the lowest club he has. South has the Ace, and expects it to win the tricks. But West has no clubs at all, and is therefore entitled to play any trump (hearts) and so win the trick, regardless of rank. He would have been permitted by the rules to discard from any other suit, but could not then have won the trick. West takes the trick, and it is now his turn to lead.

Score. Points are scored strictly in the following order:

Revoke: If a revoke has been committed, three points are added or subtracted as explained above. If, as a result, one side reaches or exceeds five points, the other may not score for tricks or honours.

Tricks: The partnership who took the majority of tricks scores one point for each trick taken above six. (Thus the win of eleven tricks is sufficient for game in one deal.)

Honours: The Ace, King, Queen and Jack of trumps are honours. If it transpires that all four were held by one partnership as the result of the deal (either all in one member's hand or distributed between them), that partnership scores four. If one partnership held three honours, it scores two. There is no score for honours if each partnership were dealt two. *Nor may a partnership score anything for honours if it stands at four points towards game.*

Game score. The partnership winning the rubber (two games) scores a bonus of two points. If three games were played, the score of the losing partnership is deducted from that of the winning partnership to determine the latter's final score.

How to play well

You cannot teach yourself to become a good Whist player, because, strictly, there is no such thing. You can only become a good Whist *partner*. We can see why as soon as we start to consider, as we must before all else, what is the whole point of the game.

You may think that whether or not you and your partner can win more tricks than your opponents depends entirely upon your luck (or lack of) in the original deal. This is not so. If in a single deal one side does happen to receive exceptionally bad cards then they probably will not win it. But in the long run the cards even themselves out and both sides get their fair share of average as well as good and bad hands. And it is the partnership that makes the better play of what they are dealt that will invariably win the majority of games.

If Whist were played with all 52 cards open to view so that everyone could see what everyone else had, the play would be purely analytical, and the game won by whichever side were better at working out all the consequences of various lines of play. It would, in technical terms, be a game of 'perfect information', like Chess.

But it is not. At the start of the first trick you know only the thirteen cards of your own hand (and the trump turn-up, which is insignificant). On the other hand, there are over six thousand million different orders in which they can be played out. You might at this point be said to have the *minimum of information* but the *maximum of flexibility*.

By the time the last trick is being played you will have learned how all 52 cards were originally distributed. But now you cannot take advantage of this knowledge, for the play of your last card is forced. At this stage, by contrast to the opening situation, you have the *maximum of information* but the *minimum of flexibility*.

During the course of the game, then, the information enabling you to make the best of your cards gradually increases from zero to 100 per cent. At the same time, your flexibility, or opportunity to take advantage of that information, gradually decreases from 100 per cent to zero. In principle, there must be a cross-over point about half way through – by the play of the seventh trick, you will have lost half your flexibility but should have acquired at least half your knowledge of the lie of cards.

In practice, however, a good partnership will play with sufficient cooperative skill to ensure that they gain as much information as possible much earlier than half way through, thereby lengthening the period of play during which they have the opportunity to take advantage of it, whereas a poor partnership will learn nothing to guide their play until it is too late. The better partnership is the one that reaches its cross-over point the sooner.

From this we draw the two fundamental lessons of good Whist play. First, it is above all a partnership game: that side wins which, all things being equal, makes the superior use of the twenty-six cards they hold between them. Second, a partnership can only hope to make superior use of its twenty-six cards if each partner plays every card not just with a view to winning the trick, but, whether he is in a position to contest the trick or not, with a view to communicating to his partner information about the cards remaining in his hand.

What sort of information has to be conveyed? Surely not a detailed account of every single card left in the hand? No – that would be impossible, and is unnecessary anyway.

How is information to be communicated? Surely not by agreeing in advance that the play of a particular card always 'means' a specific thing? Yes – more or less. That is the only way in which it can be done, and a very good system it is too.

How, then, having communicated information to each other, are you both to make maximum use of it in the play? This brings us to the whole object and strategy of the game – it is the end to which the communicative play of cards is the necessary means. And we must, of course, look first at what we are trying to do before embarking upon details of communicative play.

All this may sound pompous and long-winded and irrelevant to the enjoyment of cards. But I consider it necessary, firmly believing that you would be wasting your time if you embarked upon a game without knowing in advance what you were supposed to be trying to do. Winning the majority of tricks is only the *object* of the game. The *point* of the game is to win them by a skilfully controlled combined operation, not just by putting down your own high cards and hoping for the best.

Strategy. Unless you are exceptionally strong in trumps, which happens rarely, your normal strategy as a partnership is to establish and bring home your longest plain suit or suits. To establish a suit means to force out the high cards which your opponents hold in it (preferably by winning them in tricks, though not necessarily) so that those remaining in your hand are the highest left in play. Bringing it home means subsequently leading and winning tricks with those cards without having them trumped.

Let us illustrate the principle at work before examining how to do it. Since there are 13 cards in each suit, each player will be dealt an average of $3\frac{1}{4}$ of them. Any suit in which you hold four or more is therefore 'long' as far as you are concerned, since you have more than the average number. Those cards of it which are certain to win tricks (disregarding the possibility of trumping for the moment) are described as 'long cards'.

Suppose you have been dealt ♠A K Q 2, spades not being trumps, and the other players have an even three each. How many of these are long cards ? At first sight only the top three. But on closer inspection all four, because your lead of

$$
\begin{array}{lll}
\text{Ace draws} & 3, 4, 5 \\
\text{then King ,,} & 6, 7, 8 \\
\text{then Queen ,,} & 9, T, J
\end{array}
$$

and now no-one has any of the suit left, so your Two is bound to win if led (and not trumped). You have thus established the suit, and if you can reach a position from which you can lead the Two without having it trumped by an opponent, you will have brought the suit home.

Few holdings are as clear cut as that, of course, and you will generally need the assistance of your partner in bringing home your long suit, while he in turn will need your assistance in bringing home his. Your first task, therefore, is to let each other know what your best suit is. Normally this will be your longest suit. If you hold two long suits then strength (high cards) must be considered as well as length. Thus a holding of A K Q 2 in one suit is better than one of 6 5 4 3 2 in another, even though it is normally better to play a five-card than a four-card suit.

Opening lead. The best opportunity you have for declaring your suit is at your first lead to a trick, especially (but not solely) when by virtue of sitting immediately to the dealer's left you are responsible to the first trick of the game.

Lead from your best suit, so that your partner will know which one to return to you when he himself has the lead. And from that suit lead a card which will indicate to him what sort of holding you have in it, so that by deducting his own holding in the suit he will be able to start assembling a picture of where all the key cards are lying.

How can you choose a rank that will convey information to

him, and at the same time stand you the best possible chance of
either winning the trick immediately or at least forcing out a high
card from the opponents with a view to establishing the suit? In
response to this need, nineteenth-century experts such as
Cavendish worked out a highly complex system of codes and
conventions, to which nothing less than a treatise at least the size
of this book could be expected to do justice. Because partnership
Whist is no longer played with such intensity, and because we
are here addressing ourselves to beginners, it will be sufficient to
present the simplest account of all, as originally explained in
Foster's Whist Manual (R. F. Foster, New York, 1890).

Foster prefaced his description with a useful point to remember. It is that the most commonly led card is the King (more
than 50 per cent of the time). Therefore, look first for the King,
and if you have it be prepared to lead it – but only if you have
also a card adjacent to it, that is, either Ace or Queen. The leads
in detail are shown in Table I.

Table 1 *Which card to lead from your best plain suit*

If your best suit is headed by this:	Lead this:
A K or K Q*	King
A – Q J, or A x x x x	Ace
Q J T etc	Queen
K Q J x x	Jack
K – J T	Ten
Anything else	fourth best

*Except K Q J x x, which is the Jack lead
x means any low card, so (for example) A x x x x means 'Ace heading a
best suit of at least five cards'.

Fourth best means the fourth highest card of your suit, as, for
example, the Five from a holding of J 8 7 5 2. The reason for
this convention will become apparent later.

Table 1 is all very well, but what happens if your longest suit
is trumps? The answer depends much upon the general

strength of the hand. If you have a pretty good hand, with (say) five trumps and some high side-suit cards, lead trumps. If not, lead from your best three-card suit.

Conventional (information-giving) trump leads are shown in Table 2. There are two possible leads from a three-card suit. If it is strong (headed by the Ace, King or Queen) lead the lowest of the suit, as your partner will not go far wrong by interpreting this as the lead of fourth best from the above table. If, however, it consists of Q J x, lead the Queen, for reasons which will become obvious upon little reflection. If it is weak, lead the highest – your partner will soon deduce that you are making a 'forced lead' from his own holding in the suit or from the other cards that fall to the trick.

Table 2 *Conventional trump leads*

If your trump suit is headed by this:	Lead this:
A K Q J	J then Q
A K Q	Q then K
A K + at least 5 cards	K then A
A K + 4 or fewer	fourth best

Following your partner's lead. When your partner leads to his first trick, he will (unless returning your own suit to you) be playing from his best suit and telling you, from the card he plays, what sort of holding he has in it. His signalling will be a waste of time if you do not use your knowledge of the conventional leads, plus observation of your own cards and those that opponents play to the trick, to build up a picture of how the key cards in that suit lie. For example, if he leads a Ten and you hold the Queen, then you will realise immediately that you have K Q J T between you, and that, as soon as the Ace has been drawn from an opponent, your partner's suit is as good as established. So, before playing your own card to the trick, study his lead and make the necessary deductions. With experience, you will do this without pausing.

If he leads a high card, it is usually best to play your lowest in the suit. But be on the look-out for situations in which it is logically best, or at least a very good risk, to do otherwise. For example, suppose he leads a King and you hold the Ace and Jack. Knowing that he also has the Queen, you should play the Ace, taking the trick, and then lead the Jack, enabling him to win with the Queen. This serves the desirable purpose of leaving him in control of his best suit. If you held on to the Jack, you would then be 'blocking' him from establishing it.

If he leads a low card, indicating weakness, take the trick if you can, and with your best card – do not play clever by attempting to finesse. Again, there are conceivable exceptions, and we may note one in particular to illustrate the meaning of 'finesse'. Suppose he leads a small card, and the opponent on your right does likewise, and you hold the Ace and Queen. It is strictly correct to play the Ace, but perfectly acceptable to play the Queen instead. For if your left opponent now wins with the King, you will have the benefit of having cleared out a high adverse card while still retaining control of the suit (in the shape of the Ace); if not – there being a fair chance that the King is held by the other opponent, or even your partner – you will have made a trick with the Queen and will still retain control of the suit with the Ace. To finesse is to attempt to win a trick with a card lower than necessary. If the Queen does win, the finesse will have succeeded.

It is possible to make some valuable deductions from a low-card (fourth best) lead, and to take useful advantage of them. Foster's 'rule of eleven' is well worth applying in particular. The rule says: deduct from eleven the number of pips on the card led, and that will tell you how many higher cards lie against the leader; deduct the number of higher cards held by yourself, and that will tell you how many are held between the opponents'. Let us see it in action.

Suppose your partner leads a Seven, and second hand plays low. Seven from eleven is four, so there are four cards higher than Seven which are *not* held by your partner. Suppose you have two of them – say, Queen and Nine. Then your opponents between them hold two of the following ranks: A K J T 8. They surely hold the Ace or King, if not both, otherwise your partner would have led the King (see Table 1); equally, they cannot hold the Ace and the Eight, otherwise he would have held a suit headed by K J T and accordingly led the Ten. And so on. In this particular case you would refrain from attempting to finesse with the Queen, as there is too strong a probability that it will fall to Ace or King from the left.

If your right-hand opponent fails to follow suit to your partner's lead, don't panic – just play low and await developments.

If you hold a top sequence in the suit your partner leads, take with the lowest, in accordance with the general principle of always winning a trick as cheaply as possible.

Returning your partner's lead. If your partner led to a trick before you did, and you subsequently win a trick, then you in turn have your first lead and are immediately faced with the question whether to declare your own suit by leading from it – in accordance with the same conventions applicable to the opening lead – or to return your partner's suit.

Sometimes you can more or less do both. For instance, if your best suit is headed by A K you can lead the King and then follow with your partner's suit. The fact that the King won is enough to let him know that you also have the Ace. Thus you will have gained a trick, conveyed useful information, and kept command of your own suit, which is now known to both of you.

On principle, it is better to show your own suit before returning his, even if you lack the Ace and are likely to lose the lead; otherwise, at a later stage in the game when he has exhausted his own suit, he will have no idea what to lead for the best. You certainly must show your suit if you have reason to believe that he was making a forced lead, for to lead into such weakness would be to play into your opponents' hands. On the other hand, if you have no good suit of your own, and he has not made a forced lead from a weak three-card suit, return his immediately.

What should you lead when returning his suit? The rule is: if you have two left in the suit play the higher of them; if more, play the lowest. Why? If you have two, and play high before low, your partner will know by convention that you have none left in the suit. Furthermore, if your higher card is significantly high – say Ten or better – then by playing it you remove the risk of blocking his suit and so preventing him from establishing it. If, however, you have three or more, you must have been dealt the suit long to start with (having already released one to the trick he led in it). In this case the suit is good for both of you, and the need to unblock is less urgent – though you can still do so by playing high to a subsequent trick as required.

If your partner led from trumps, return your lowest.

Playing second to a trick. Play low, unless you know for certain that you can win the trick. Do not try to compete for it: this is the job of your partner, who will have the advantage of playing last and knowing what he has to beat, whereas you would be playing speculatively. If, however, there has as yet been no sign of the Ace, and you hold the King and Queen, by all means attempt a finesse by playing the Queen: you will either win the trick, which is good, or be left with the commanding card, which is also good. There are those who would play the King when holding neither Ace nor Queen. This is a risk that may or may not be worth taking.

If you are void in the suit and do not know whether or not your partner is able to win the trick, should you ruff it or not, on the off-chance? This depends on your trump holding. If it is weak, then the best use you can make of your small trumps is to attempt all reasonable ruffs; if strong, pass it up. You can afford to lose the trick if you have strength in trumps for later play, where trumps come into their own, while, by discarding from a side-suit, you not only get rid of a useless card but also convey potentially useful information to your partner about the rest of your hand.

Playing third to a trick. In this position you are either leading your own suit or returning your partner's, as previously described. You should attempt to win the trick if your partner is not already doing so.

Playing fourth to a trick. In this position your only job is to take the trick if your partner has not already won it, and the only logical requirement for you is to play the lowest you can for either purpose. Be it noted that the rule about winning a trick as cheaply as possible applies even when you are playing from a sequence. For instance, if you are playing fourth to a trick containing (improbably) the Two, Three and Four of a suit, and you hold (say) Seven, Eight and Nine, play the Seven. It is true that any card of a sequence is as good as any of its fellows for trick-taking purposes, but for the purposes of conveying information, the fact that you are known to be playing the lowest can be of considerable significance to your partner.

Discarding. When you are void and prefer not to trump, choose carefully which suit to discard from. It is not right to look merely for the lowest-ranking card regardless of suit, and it is positively wrong to discard from your longest suit or the one you are trying to establish. Prefer to throw the lowest card from your weakest suit. But consider this example: you have the choice of discarding from A Q 2 in one suit or T 9 3 in another. Here it is better to throw the Two, for reasons which you should be able to work out for yourself.

Trumps. If you have five or more trumps, lead them, unless they are all very low and you have a well-headed plain suit. Do not lead trumps if you have only four, although if they include two honours and you have no other clear lead, you may be justified in leading trumps (low).

If you have such strength but do not have the lead, you may still find an opportunity to call for them by the way in which you play to other tricks. The call for trumps – a signal known as the Blue Peter – consists in playing an unnecessarily high card in a given suit, and then following it with one lower at the suit's next appearance. We have already seen something similar at work in the situation where, holding two only of your partner's suit, you return the higher of them first: when you play the second, you thereby indicate that you are void in the suit, and are in a position to trump if it comes round again. The fact that you are not necessarily void in the suit being used for the Blue Peter does not militate against its communicative value: the fact that your partner sees you play high then low should alert him to the fact that you are ready to play in trumps.

There is also the question of forcing trumps, which means leading a suit in which you know somebody else is void. You should always force if you know that your opponents are strong in trumps, for, if effective, this reduces the power left against the establishment of your own suits as well as against your own trumps when trump tricks are led. If the opponents refuse to be drawn, keep on forcing until they dare not do otherwise than to ruff.

You may also force your partner, but only if you are strong in trumps yourself.

Sample games

In the following four deals you are presented, as the player designated South, with the hand of cards from which you play. The other cards – including your partner's (North) – are not fully revealed until the end of the hand. Instead, we take each trick one by one, show what cards are played by your partner and your opponents, and consider your own contribution on the basis only of what can be seen at the time, or deduced from what has gone before. In other words, each deal is described from the viewpoint of you, South, as if in the course of actual play. For the sake of variety and to demonstrate all playing positions, you lead to the first trick in the first deal and thereafter the opening leads come respectively from West, from North and from East.

The deals themselves demonstrate both elementary and advanced lines of play, and are adapted from examples originally provided by the great player Cavendish. You will find it well worth your while to deal the opening hand described, lay the remaining 39 cards face up to one side, and follow each trick through by playing out the cards specified. The winning card of each trick is printed in bold type.

First deal. East deals, turning up ♣J as the trump card, and you have the opening lead to make from the following hand:

♠A Q J T 2   ♡Q 6   ♣A 9 8 3   ♢9 3

Your best suit – the one which you will try to establish, and from which you will lead – is spades. You have some strength in trumps, which is enhanced by the fact that you have two (red) suits of below average length and may therefore be expected to make two tricks by ruffing. It is a pity that your red Queen is unguarded: with two lower cards instead of one she might have been expected to win the third round of hearts.

Trick 1

S	♠ A	A clear cut example of an Ace lead. You tell North
W	♠ 5	that this is the suit you would like returned, and that
N	♠ 4	you have in it high cards lacking the King. A run of
E	♠ 3	low spades played to your lead suggests that the suit is fairly evenly distributed.

Trick 2

S	♠ J	Continue the suit, hoping to draw the King – which
W	♠ 6	in fact you do, leaving your Queen high. (You will
N	♠ 8	ask why Jack is led from the sequence Q J T – isn't
E	♠ K	Queen the right card to lead ? Yes, it is. The answer here is that in Cavendish's full-blown signalling system the lead of Ace then Jack shows that your complete holding was A Q J T and none lower. I have avoided 'correcting' the lead, in order to indicate the subtleties of which the game is capable.

Trick 3

E	♦ 6	Now your right-hand opponent leads what is
S	♦ 3	presumably the fourth best of his best suit, though
W	♦ K	not a strong one. As second to the trick, it is proper
N	♦ 2	for you to play low. The fact that West takes it with the King suggests that he also holds the Ace, otherwise he would not risk losing it to your partner.

Trick 4

W	♦ A	West returns his partner's suit, in preference to
N	♦ 5	opening one of his own, so presumably does not
E	♦ 4	have another certain trick in the form of an Ace. You
S	♦ 9	have only the Nine left, and are ready to ruff if diamonds are led again.

Trick 5

W	♡ 4	But he switches suits – and to your surprise gives
N	♡ 3	you a trick with your unguarded Queen.
E	♡ J	Presumably hearts are West's best suit. So far your
S	♡ Q!	partner has not been able to communicate with you, but from his play so far he does not appear to have anything exciting to offer.

Trick 6

Now it is your lead again, and your hand is ♠Q T 2, ♡6, ♣A 9 7 3. With the command in spades, a void in diamonds and some ruffing strength to match, you are now well placed to see about drawing some trumps with a view to the ultimate bringing home of your spades. The fact that your opponents have switched suits, yet neither led nor called for trumps, suggests that they are not too well off in that suit. So:

S	♣ 3	You lead low, in accordance with principle. Second-
W	♣ 6	hand plays low, as he ought; your partner competes
N	♣Q	for the trick, as is proper; and East, by playing what
E	♣ 4	is presumably his lowest, demonstrates that the King does not lie with him. Therefore either West or North has it. And North, at last, can lead to you.

Trick 7

N	♣ 7	This trick, exactly half way through the play, tells
E	♣ 5	you everything you need to know! The only trumps
S	♣ A	now left in play against you are King, Jack and Two.
W	♣ T	East has the Jack, because you saw it turned as trump indicator. Your partner, North, must hold the Two and that *alone*. If it were held by either opponent, it would have appeared as the lowest card at Trick 6 (assuming, as you must, that everyone plays properly). And if North held K 7 2 at the start of this trick, instead of just 7 and 2, he should have led the latter. Unnecessarily playing high before low is nearly always a signal that the two cards concerned are the only ones held in their particular suit. It now follows that West has ♣K,

and you therefore have two trumps to everyone else's one. So now you can draw them out preparatorily to bringing home your spades.

Trick 8

S	♠ 8
W	♣ K
N	♣ 2
E	♣ J

The trick falls as expected, leaving you with ♠Q T 2, ♡6, ♣9. With winning spades and the only trump in play, all you can lose is ♡6 to a top heart. If West leads spades you capture, lead the other two to win, then make your last trump before throwing your Six to the Ace of hearts. If West leads anything else you trump it, then lead spades as before. Whichever way it goes, you score three for tricks, taking nine out of the thirteen.

The deal in full at the start of the game was:

North: ♠84 ♡A753 ♣Q72 ◇J852
East: ♠K73 ♡J9 ♣J54 ◇QT764
West: ♠965 ♡KT842 ♣KT6 ◇AK

Second deal. And now you deal, turning up ♠8 for trumps and finding yourself lying fourth to the first trick on the following hand:

♠98 ♡AQ654 ♣QT ◇J653

This time you are definitely weak in trumps, and have only one good suit, the hearts. And once again, you have an unguarded Queen, for which you might compensate by ruffing the third round of clubs. West is to lead.

Trick 1

W	♣ 4
N	♣ 5
E	♣ 9
S	♣ T

As happened in the previous deal, you are surprised to take a trick as cheaply as this. Presumably clubs are West's best suit but he lacks the Ace; and, presumably, from the result, your partner must have it.

Trick 2

S	♣ Q	You ought really to declare your hearts by leading
W	♣ K	the Ace, but this club lead is not meaningless, as
N	♣ A	your partner ought to infer that you are voiding the
E	♣ 7	suit. As it happens, the result, which squeezes a
		King out of the opponents, is better than you might
		expect.

Trick 3

N	♡ 7	Now it is your partner's first lead and opportunity
E	♡ 8	to communicate – and, to your surprise, hearts is his
S	♡ Q	best suit as well as yours; if he has led the fourth
W	♡ J	best of it, which is probable but not absolutely
		certain, then he must have K T 9 left, giving your
		side command of the suit. The only trouble is that
		your own shortness of trumps suggests that you will
		be lucky to bring the suit home. You have now to
		lead from ♠ 9 8 ♡ A 7 5 4 ◊ J 6 5 3.

Trick 4

S	◊ 3	You are not in a position to lead trumps, nor do you
W	◊ 7	wish to have your hearts ruffed. This leaves only
N	◊ A	diamonds to lead from; if pursued further, they may
E	◊ 4	draw some trumps.

Trick 5

N	◊ T	Partner avoids hearts too, presumably for the same
E	◊ K	reason, and seems equally disinclined to lead
S	◊ 5	trumps. His high-ranking lead suggests that he may
W	◊ 8	be voiding the suit in order to ruff it.

Trick 6

E	♠ Q	It is East's first lead, and out come his big guns –
S	♠ 8	trumps are called for. West appears to have the Ace,
W	♠ K	which bodes ill. Your partner's lowest trump is the
N	♠ 3	Three, so he may have several others.

Trick 7

W	♠ A
N	♠ 4
E	♠ 2
S	♠ 9

So far, so bad; and your last trump has been sounded. Five are left in play – J T 7 6 5 – and of these East must have at least the Jack and Ten to have led the Queen to the previous trick. North probably has two of the others.

Trick 8

W	♣ J
N	♠ 6
E	♣ 6
S	♡ 4

Now that *is* interesting. West must be out of trumps to have led as he did, and North has been able to turn a trump to his advantage.

Trick 9

N	♡ 2
E	♡ 3
S	♡ 5
W	♣ 2

An unexpected pleasure: East was obliged to follow suit with what little he had, and West was void in trumps as well as hearts, and so you win with a small one.

Trick 10

And here we are at the crux of the deal. You have to lead from ♡A 6, ◇J 6. Should you now make with the Ace? No! East is sure to trump it, and cannot lead anything to your good. Consider the position. North, you know (from Trick 3), has three hearts, no clubs, and either a trump or a diamond as his fourth card. If his fourth card is the diamond, then East must have four trumps (West being void), and East will take all no matter what you lead. But if his fourth card is a trump (spade), you can force it by playing into his void suit. Therefore:

S	◇ 6!
W	◇ 9
N	♠ 7
E	◇ 2

You lead diamonds, and your partner scores his last trump to give you the odd (seventh) trick. East, of course, wins the final three – but they are not the ones that count.

The other hands were:

North	♠7 6 4 3 ♡K T 9 7 2 ♣A 5 ◇A T
East	♠Q J T 5 2 ♡8 3 ♣9 7 6 ◇K 4 2
West	♠A K ♡J ♣K J 8 4 3 2 ◇Q 9 8 7

Third deal. Your partner deals you the following hand, turns up
♡6 and leads:

    ♠A Q J ♡A K 9 3 ♣J 8 6 2 ◊J 5

This is a hand from which you are glad not to have the opening
lead: its longest plain suit (clubs) is weak, and its strongest plain
suit (spades) in short, while the strongest suit is trumps (hearts),
and far from outstanding at that.

Trick 1

N   ◊ K   Diamonds are your partner's best friend, and he
E   ◊ 8   appears to have a good holding headed by A K or
S   ◊ 5   K Q. Your own shortness in the suit is a strength
W   ◊ 4   rather than a weakness – but East's 'lowest card' as
               second to the trick looks dangerously high. He also
               may be playing from a two-card holding, in which
               case he will be ruffing diamonds at their third
               appearance, and you will have to overtrump.

Trick 2

N   ◊ A   A second trick in the suit, and it is clear to North
E   ◊ Q   that both you and East are out of it. You can now
S   ♠ J   expect him to lead a different plain suit – or might he
W   ◊ 7   turn to trumps ?

Trick 3

N   ♠ T   Your favourite suit. From your own holding it
E   ♠ 3   seems likely that your partner is leading the top of a
S   ♠ J   three-card suit. And from your holding of A Q J it is
W   ♠ 2   natural to finesse against the King by playing the
               Jack. The finesse succeeds: West does not have the
               King. Neither does North, for he would not have
               led the Ten from King, Ten alone, while from
               King, Ten and small he would have led the smallest.
               So East must have the King. Naturally, it would
               have been foolish for him to play it second to the
               trick.

Trick 4

S	♡ 3
W	♡ 6
N	♡ J
E	♡ 5

You now have your first lead, and hold ♠A Q ♡A K 9 3 ♣J 8 6 2. Your best suit is trumps, and it is not brilliant, so you lead it low. (You might have played ♠A, but would then leave East's King in command of the suit.) West has probably played from a pair of high hearts, and either he or your partner has the Queen.

Trick 5

N	♡ 4
E	♡ 8
S	♡ K
W	♡ 7

North returns trumps, as he ought, and you are tempted to slip over East's Eight with your Nine. But as third hand you are morally obliged to play high, and there is an outside chance that you will catch a Queen from West.

Trick 6

S	♡ A
W	♡ T
N	♡ 2
E	♠ 4

You ought now to turn to another suit, but it seems worth while to seek to draw the Queen of trumps. Unfortunately, she lies with West, as it is clear from the cards that your partner is now out of trumps. Remember that he returned the Four to you in the previous trick, and has now gone down with the Two: 'high then low' is the correct play from a holding of two, so he must now be void. No doubt you interpreted his previous lead of the Four as lower rather than higher.

Trick 7

You must now lead from ♠A Q , ♡9, ♣J 8 6 2. Your side has six tricks, and you need only play the top spade to make your seventh. Yet there may still be a way to make your trump as well – bearing in mind that every overtrick counts a point towards game – and to compensate for your previous rashness in hearts. It is obvious that your opponents have a trick or three to make in clubs, so you can afford to let them start their little fling:

S	♣ 2	North attempts to make his King, but the chances
W	♣ 3	are 50/50 in theory, and in practice East makes it
N	♣ K	100 to 0 against by overtaking with the Ace. This
E	♣ A	gives you a slight advantage, in that your Jack is now

second highest in the suit, instead of only third in
line of succession.

Trick 8

E	♣ Q	The Queen comes out, and now your Jack is high.
S	♣ 6	
W	♣ 7	
N	♣ 5	

Trick 9

E	♣ 4	You have your odd trick, unexpectedly in clubs –
S	♣ J	thanks to your 'guarded Jack' and the fall of Ace and
W	♣ T	King to the same trick.
N	◇ 3	

Trick 10

You to lead again, from ♠A Q, ♡9, ♣8. Key cards against you
are ♣9, held by East, ♠K, also held by East, and ♡Q, held by
West. (If ♣9 were held by West, he would have just played it
instead of the Ten. For the placing of the other two, see Tricks
3 and 6.) Since East is void in diamonds (Trick 2) and West has
the only other trump, East must have three spades with his club.
If you force East to lead, he will have to play spades right into
your hands, for his King can only win if led into. Then either
you make two spades, or West trumps one of them and you make
a spade and the other trump. And you *can* force East to lead, as
follows:

		Trick 11		*Trick 12*		*Trick 13*	
S	♣ 8	E	♠ 5	W	◇ T	S	♠ A
W	♠ 6	S	♠ Q	N	◇ 6	W	◇ 9
N	◇ 2	W	♡ Q	E	◇ 8	N	♠ 9
E	♣ 9	N	♠ 7	S	♡ 6	E	♠ K

So you finish with a score of three for tricks, having taken nine
in all. The other hands prove to have been:

```
North    ♠T 9 7  ♡K 4 2  ♣K 5  ◇A K 6 3 2
East     ♠K 8 5 4 3  ♡8 5  ♣A Q 9 4  ◇Q 8
West     ♠6 2  ♡Q T 7 6  ♣T 7 3  ◇T 9 7 4
```

Fourth deal. Your partner, North, deals you the following hand, and turns up ◇5. You will be playing second hand to East's opening lead.

♠4 ♡A K Q T 2 ♣8 7 ◇K T 8 7 3

You are immediately struck by the uneven distribution (5–5–2–1), and must be prepared for the whole deal to be unbalanced. Your strong heart suit, for instance could be ruffed at the first round. Fortunately, you are also strong in trumps, and that is really what counts.

Trick 1

E	◇ 6	Well, well. East's best suit appears to be trumps too.
S	◇ 3	And since North could not overtake West's Jack,
W	◇ J	both Ace and Queen must lie with the opponents –
N	◇ 5	very probably with East.

Trick 2

W	◇ 2	West dutifully returns his partner's suit, and, to
N	♣ 2	your disappointment but not to your great surprise,
E	◇ A	your own partner proves trumpless. Note, however,
S	◇ 7	the suit of his discard: his best suit must be clubs. East, properly, played high, leaving your King in command of the trump suit for the time being. You now expect a change of policy from East. . .

Trick 3

E	♠ 3	The lead is presumably of East's second best suit,
S	♠ 4	and not a very good one. Your partner finds an Ace
W	♠ Q	to compensate for his lack of trumps, and is now
N	♠ A	placed with the lead.

Trick 4

N	♣ A	As you suspected from Trick 2, your partner's suit
E	♣ K	is clubs, and it is a strong one, as his lead indicates.
S	♣ 7	But the unevenness of the distribution strikes again,
W	♣ 3	for East's response clearly shows that his King was single.

Trick 5

N	♣ J	North must be as aware, as you are, that East will
E	◇ 4	trump; the fact that he pursues his clubs neverthe-
S	♣ 8	less indicates considerable length in the suit.
W	♣4	

Trick 6

E	♠ 2	East resumes his quest in spades, and at last you can
S	◇ 8	take the initiative. North will be observing your
W	♠ 7	lead with interest.
N	♠ 6	

Trick 7

You have the lead from ♡A K Q T 2, ◇K T, and both sides have taken three tricks. Hearts, your strong suit, have not yet been played. You are well placed in trumps, holding K T against Q 9, which latter you can place with East. (He must have held five trumps to have legitimately opened them to the first trick.) You must lead from the hearts, otherwise you give East a trick in trumps either now or later. By leading from the top down, you are bound to make the four (at least) you need for game, for as soon as East trumps a heart, both your trumps will win.

Effectively, therefore, the play may be said to end at this point. But Cavendish, not liking to take the easy way out of anything, goes on to show how you can be virtually certain of taking all the remaining tricks between yourself and North!

His argument is based on the knowledge, from certain conventions of play, that East led originally from a holding of five spades (though even if he had led from four, as you yourself can surmise from the play, the following approach would still be correct). That being so, East must have three spades left in hand, plus his two trumps, no clubs (see Trick 4), and therefore not more than two of the outstanding hearts. So he will start ruffing when you reach the Queen. Your partner, however, has a long line of clubs. If East can be induced to drop a trump on a club lead, you yourself can overtrump – preventing him from making another trick. Therefore:

	Trick 8		*Trick* 9		*Trick* 10
S ♡ 2!	N ♣ Q	N ♣ T	N ♣ 6
W ♡ 5	E ♠ 5	E ♡ 8	E ♠ J
N ♡ 9	S ♡ T	S ♡ Q	S ♡ K
E ♡ 7	W ♣ 9	W ♡ 6	W ♡ J

Trick 11	*Trick* 12	*Trick* 13
N ♣ 5	N ♡ 4	S ◇ K
E ♠ 9	E ◇ 9	W ♠ K
S ♡ A	S ◇ T	N ♡ 3
W ♠ 8	W ♠ T	E ◇ Q

The play of these last few tricks shows the power of position. If at any point during North's club leads East had attempted to take with a trump, you would merely have overtaken with the next higher trump, led out your next trump to win his last, and then pursued the hearts in complete safety. So long as he feared to do this, you remained quite happy to throw your ♡A K Q T trick-winning cards to your partner's uncontested ♣Q T 6 5.

The other hands were :

North   ♠A 6 ♡9 4 3 ♣A Q J T 6 5 2 ◇5
East   ♠J 9 5 3 2 ♡8 7 ♣K ◇A Q 9 6 4
West   ♠K Q T 8 7 ♡J 6 5 ♣9 4 3 ◇J 2

The potential depth of Whist may not be to everybody's taste, and there is no reason why it should be. But I hope the examples given above are enough to show what scope the game gives for brilliant play, and why, before the advent of Bridge, Whist was universally regarded as one of the great games of the world. It is also the most basic of all trick-taking games, being easy to learn without any previous knowledge of card play. Once play Whist, and you can approach any new card game with complete confidence.

A contract is an undertaking to do something. The chief difference between Whist and Contract Whist is that, instead of playing the tricks out and then seeing, as a matter of interest, which side has taken the majority, one side at the start of the game *undertakes* to win a certain minimum number of tricks. In return for this undertaking, the contracting side has the privilege of nominating as trumps the suit which will best help them to achieve their objective. Both sides have the opportunity to compete for the right to name trumps and make a contract, which they do by means of an auction. The side achieving the contract is the one that makes the highest bid – that is, which quotes the highest number of tricks as their target.

Developed in the 1930s by Hubert Phillips, Contract Whist is perhaps best characterised as a cross between Whist and Contract Bridge. It can advance certain claims to superiority over both, yet has singularly failed to attract the popularity of either. (For which reason, one might further characterise it as a good game for good Liberals.) Over Whist, as we have seen, it has two particular advantages: the trump suit is not determined by chance, but is arrived at by the skilled process of bidding, which thus becomes the primary means by which partners communicate information about their hands to each other; and the objective is not always the same – instead of both sides always trying to make at least seven tricks, one side (contracting) is trying to make whatever higher number they may have bid, while the other (defending) is trying to stop them. Thus if the contractors have guaranteed to take at least eight, they need at least eight to win, whereas the defenders need only six to beat them.

If you already know Contract Bridge, you may wonder what on earth Contract Whist can advance as a claim to rivalry with it. Well, consider the following.

First, there is no dummy. Everyone plays with his own hand of cards, concealed, as in all proper card games.

Second, the scoring system is simple. It gives credit for winning tricks, not for amassing points.

Third, such over-elaborations are eliminated as scoring for honours, which gives credit where none is due; slam premiums, which tend to bias the logical progression of the bidding; and the vulnerability factor, whose object of inhibiting over-confident speculation is nullified by the converse sin of sacrifice bidding.

Fourth, it is not played by fanatics.

The game

Cards. A standard 52-card pack. (Or two used alternately, one being shuffled while the other is dealt.)

Preliminaries. Decide partnerships and the first dealer by any agreed means. Scores are noted on a sheet divided by a vertical line into two columns, one for each side, and by a horizontal line about half way down (see illustration). Bonuses are entered above this line, and scores towards game are entered below it. A game is won by the first side to score ten or more points below the line, which may take one or several deals to achieve. The match, or rubber, ends as soon as one side has won two games, and is won by the side with the higher total score for games and bonuses.

Shuffle and deal. Anyone may shuffle, but the dealer has the right to shuffle last. Deal the whole pack out in ones, face down, until everyone has thirteen cards.

Object. There is a round of competitive bidding between the four players to determine which side will make a contract and nominate the trump suit. The object of the contracting side is then to make at least the number of tricks they bid, and the object of their opponents is to prevent them from doing so.

If the opponents think they will beat the contractors, they may, before play begins, double the score to be made by whichever side wins the round. If they do so, the contractors themselves may redouble – i.e. quadruple the score to be made.

The auction. Dealer is the first to speak. He may make any bid, or pass by saying 'no bid'. Continuing clockwise around the table, each player in turn must either make a higher bid than one that has gone before, or pass by saying 'no bid'. A player who has once passed is not debarred from bidding when his turn comes round again. As soon as a bid has been followed by three consecutive passes, the last-named bid becomes the contract and determines the trump suit (if any) and the number of tricks being contested. If all players pass before any bid is made, the deal is abandoned and the next deal made by the player on the present dealer's left.

The bids. Each bid proposes an undertaking to win one or more tricks than six. Thus a bid of one claims to win seven tricks, a bid of two means eight, and so on to a maximum of seven, which is a bid to win all thirteen. A bid for a higher number beats or 'overcalls' any bid for a lower number.

Each bid consists of a number plus either the name of the suit being offered as trumps or the announcement 'no trumps'. The suits themselves rank in a bidding or pecking order, so that a bid in one suit may be overcalled by a bid of the same number but in a higher-ranking suit. From lowest to highest, they are:

♣	clubs
◇	diamonds
♡	hearts
♠	spades
NT	no trumps

(*Examples:* The lowest bid of all is 'one club', which we write '1 ♣'. This may be overcalled by 'one' anything else. But 1 ♠ can only be overcalled by 1NT, or by a higher number of anything else, and 1 NT can only be followed by something in a higher number. Similarly, 2 ♡ is overcalled by 2 ♠, 2 NT, then 3 ♣, and so on. The highest bid of all is 7 NT – an offer to win all thirteen tricks with no trump suit.)

Doubling. Whenever it is your turn to speak, you may, instead of bidding or no-bidding, say 'double' to the previous bid (provided that it was made by an opponent, not your partner). And if the opponent on your right has just doubled (or the opponent on your left did so and was followed by two passes), you yourself may redouble.

Although a call of double or redouble does not advance the bidding level, neither does it count as a pass, and either call must be followed by three consecutive passes to establish the (re-)doubled bid as the final contract.

If, however, a double or redouble is followed by another positive bid, it is thereby cancelled, and everyone pretends it was a pass.

Example of auction (To be skipped if everything is crystal clear)

South	West	North	East
1 ♡	no	1 ♠	1 NT

Suits follow in pecking order, West passes.

no	no	2 ♡	dble

South dislikes spades; East doubles hearts

3 ♡	dble	re-d	no

South responds to his partner's re-bid in his own suit, thereby cancelling the double; West, somewhat improbably, doubles again, thinking that if his partner thinks they can beat a 2 ♡ contract then he himself thinks they can beat one of 3 ♡; North redoubles because he is quite sure that he and his partner can win; East passes. The last bid was followed by three passes or equivalents, so the last-named bid is the contract. North and South are playing to win at least nine tricks (6+3 bid) with hearts as trumps. East and West will beat them if they can take five tricks themselves. (This is not an example of good bidding.)

The play. The opening lead is made by the opponent sitting to the left of the declarer (i.e. of the member of the contracting partnership who first named the suit of the contract being played. In the above example, the lead would be made by West. If North had passed instead of switching to 2 ♡, the contract would have been 1 NT by East-West and the opening lead made by South.)

The usual rules of trick-taking apply. You must follow suit to the card led if possible; if not, you may trump (if any) or discard. The trick is taken with the highest card of the suit led, or the highest trump if any are played. The winner of a trick leads to the next. (For convenience, one member of each partnership keeps together the tricks made by himself and his partner.) All hands are played out – do not cease play once the contract has been made or broken.

Scoring. If the contract is fulfilled, the contracting side makes a contract score below the line, which counts towards game; and if they make any tricks over and above their contract ('overtricks') they score a bonus which is entered above the line but does not count towards game. If the contract is defeated, the opponents get a premium for each trick by which the contractors fell short of their contract, and this is entered above the line in their column.

The actual scores are as follows:

Scoring factor	Un-D	Dbld	Re-D
TO CONTRACTING SIDE IF CONTRACT MADE:		*below*	
For each contracted trick if a NO-TRUMP contract	4	8	16
For each contracted trick if in a SUIT contract	3	6	12
		above	
For each overtrick (whether in suit or no trumps)	2	5	10
Special bonus for fulfilling a doubled contract	—	5	10
TO OPPONENTS IF CONTRACT BEATEN:			
For each undertrick	10	20	40
FOR WINNING THE RUBBER: a bonus of	50	—	—

NS	EW
6	10
6	20
6	
12	
	12
9	8
	3
	50
39	103

FIGURE 2

Scoresheet at Contract Whist is divided by a horizontal line as
at Contract Bridge (for which printed score-pads are available
from many stationers). Scores towards game are entered below
the line, bonuses above it. This illustration shows the score-
sheet for the sample game given later. N–S win the first deal by
succeeding in a suit-bid of two odd tricks (score 6). They lose
the second by falling short of their contract by two, allowing
E–W to score 20 above the line. They win the third by making a
contract of four (score 12) with three over-tricks (6 above the
line). Thus N–S win the first game, and a second horizontal
line is drawn. E–W win the second game in one deal, bidding
two in suit, doubled, and taking one over-trick, to score 12
below the line, 5 above for the doubled over-trick, plus 5 above
for the doubled game bonus. The third game is hard fought,
but after three deals E–W win and add in the 50 bonus for
winning the rubber.

Scores made above the line continue to be entered throughout the rubber and are not totalled or ruled off until it ends.

Scores made below the line are best entered separately (rather than added cumulatively). As soon as one side has reached or exceeded a total of ten points below the line – which may take one or several deals – the first game ends and another horizontal line is ruled under the game score. The second game then begins, each side starting again with a score of zero below the second line. As before, scores made for successfully contracted tricks are entered below the (second) line, and all others continued above the first.

If the two sides win a game each, a third line is drawn and the same procedure followed. As soon as one side has won two games, it enters a bonus of 50. All the scores in each column are then totalled (all above- as well as below-line figures), and the side with the higher aggregate wins. Settlement may be made on the basis of the margin between the two totals.

Hints on play

Whereas in Whist the exchange of useful information between the partners is carried out entirely by the deliberately communicative choice of cards to play to tricks, or what might be called 'playing conventions', in Contract Whist, as in Bridge, most of the information is exchanged during the auction – that is, before any cards are actually revealed – by means of what are in effect 'bidding conventions'.

These hints on play concentrate on the bidding, since it is assumed that you are already acquainted with ordinary Whist. The bidding is substantially the same as that used for Bridge, but I write on the assumption that you do not already play Bridge, and you may well find these notes helpful if you turn later to that more popular game.

(If you *do* already play Bridge, use for Contract Whist whatever system you are accustomed to. But there are one or two points of difference between the two games which you might profitably keep in mind if you are using normal Bridge bidding. First, the fact that declarer does not play from an exposed hand makes any given contract that much harder to fulfil in Contract Whist. Second, the fact that there are no 'slam bonuses' means that the bidding, as Phillips put it in his book '*Contract Whist*', 'is not conditioned by the desirability of building up to a slam feature'. Third, the scoring system makes sacrifice bidding less worth while. Fourth, there is no distinction between major and minor suits. Thus ten tricks in any suit will produce game from nothing, and some bidding conventions whose significance may turn on the major/minor distinction (e.g. Stayman) have no important place in Contract Whist.)

Introduction to bidding. The purpose of bidding is not to outdo one another in betting on who has the best hand. It is for you and your partner to describe your holdings to each other with a view to arriving at a contract that will suit you both – or on agreeing to pass if you have none. You do this by stages and usually in small steps, not necessarily sticking to the same suit at each bid.

In order to make a bid you must have some good reason for believing that you and your partner can take a majority of tricks – that is, at least seven between you. To make this minimum of seven, one of you must take at least four tricks. Since you cannot speak for your partner, you can only reasonably bid if you can see four tricks in your own hand, assuming that your best suit is made trumps.

Assessing how many tricks your hand is worth will come naturally if you already play Whist or something similar. To recap, consider the following hand:

> ♠ A 9 6
> ♡ K Q 4
> ◇ Q 2
> ♣ Q T 8 3 2

How many tricks is it worth ? So long as the total distribution is not freakishly adverse, you may assess the hand as follows:

In spades, the Ace will win whether the suit is led by you or anyone else. Count 1 trick.

In hearts, the King and Queen will win two tricks after someone has led the Ace and you have thrown the Four to it, leaving your monarchs in command of the suit. Count 2 tricks; total 3 so far.

In diamonds the Queen will lose because she is unguarded: after throwing the Two to the lead of the Ace she will be carried off by the lead of the King. Count 0 tricks; total still 3 so far.

In clubs the Queen is guarded several times over. Theoretically you throw the Two to the Ace and the Three to the King, and the Queen is then in command. But there is a snag. With five of the suit in your hand, at least one other player is bound to hold not more than two. If that player is an opponent, he will be out of the suit by the time he has played to the Ace and the King, and will therefore be able to trump your Queen. On this basis, then, you still have a total of only 3 tricks.

Unless, of course, clubs are trumps. Now this radically alters the situation. First of all, your short holding in diamonds is no longer a weakness, for after the Ace and King have gone you can ruff the third diamond lead with your lowest club. That's one extra trick. And in clubs themselves, you can throw the Three and the Eight to the Ace and King, after which your Queen is the top trump for another certain trick, and the Ten another possible winner.

With clubs as trumps, then, you can see a good five tricks in your own hand. Assuming, as you must until you hear otherwise, that your partner can produce the average three from his own hand, you have eight tricks between you and a bid of up to 2♣ or even 3♣.

This hand illustrates the general principle that in order to bid, you need a certain amount of strength (high-ranking cards) and a biddable suit (in effect, one with at least four and preferably more cards in your hand). You can dispense with a biddable suit if you have strength in all four suits sufficient to justify a bid at no trumps.

	(a)	(b)	(c)	(d)
♠	Q J x x	A K x x x	A K x x	x x x x x
♡	K Q x	Q J x x	A Q x	Q x x x
◇	Q 3 2	J x	K x x	J x
♣	K 3 2	x x	A K x	Q x

On the opposite page are shown various patterns of strength and distribution from the viewpoint of the opening bid. (x) denotes any card lower than Jack – the exact denominations are irrelevant to the principle. (a) shows a balanced distribution (4–3–3–3) and no biddable suit. It counts 11 strength points (as will be explained below), and is not strong enough to open (though it will provide strong support for any bid from partner). (b) also counts 11 strength points, but adds two for the uneven distribution. There is no doubt about the biddable suit: open the bidding with 'one spade'. (c) has the same balanced distribution as (a), counting no distribution points, but is considerably strengthened, counting 23. This calls for a no-trump bid. With six or seven clear tricks in our own hand, open 'two no trump'. (d) has the same unbalanced distribution as (b) but is clearly so weak as to be unbiddable.

An elementary but reliable method of measuring both strength and distribution is that of the point-count system, which is simple to apply. You merely count points for all the high cards you hold as follows:

Ace   4
King   3
Queen   2
Jack   1

There being 40 points in the pack, you have only an average deal if your count for honours is a bare ten. If you have as many as 20, you have half the strength of the pack in your hand alone.

For distribution, you count as follows:

3 for a void (no cards in a particular suit)
2 for a singleton (only one in a suit)
1 for a doubleton (only two in a suit)

If the cards are distributed completely evenly between the players (4–3–3–3 per player) no-one will have distribution points to count. On the other hand, if you have a markedly unbalanced distribution, then at least one other player must have distribution points to count as well. So although these add to your absolute strength, they do not necessarily add to your comparative strength. In any case, distribution points are only of value when there is a trump suit.

To make an opening bid, your hand should be worth at least 13 points. Let's go back to the first hand (page 37) and see how it measures up. Ace, King and three Queens make up the requisite minimum. Furthermore you have a doubleton in diamonds, which increases your count by one. For practice, you may like to measure the strength of hands (a) to (d) to see how they shape up for an opening bid.

Having referred twice to an 'opening' bid, I must now point out the significance of the term.

If you are the first member of your partnership to speak at the auction, any bid you make is an opening bid. But if you are the second to speak, and your partner has made the opening bid, any bid that you come back with is a 'responsive' bid. The reason for distinguishing between the two is obvious. When you make an opening bid, you are in complete ignorance of your partner's hand and can therefore speak only for yourself. Any suit you name must be good for trumps. But when you make a responsive bid, you have already heard something from your partner about the state of his hand. Your bid must therefore be made in the light of two hands rather than one. The suit you name may not be good for trumps, but may be good for his support; you therefore make it on the assumption that he will not leave you in it, but will come back at his next turn and make a re-bid.

Conversely, as the opener, you must be prepared to bid a second time if your partner responds to your first. It is for this reason that you (usually) start the bidding at below your maximum strength, so as to leave room for expansion on the re-bid, and that you need the above-average point count of 13.

At this point, then, we must start to consider opening and responsive bids separately. There is, of course, a complication introduced by the fact that your opponents may also be bidding and so preventing you from proceeding in small, communicative steps by forcing you to make higher bids than they do if you want to stay in. We shall just have to ignore this, and assume that they keep passing, in order to make any progress at all.

Opening bids. Only open the bidding if you have at least 13 points and either a biddable suit or well-distributed strength in all (for no trumps). The fact that you open at all, in a trump suit, is to be taken as a guarantee to your partner that you will make a re-bid if he responds – so avoid bidding if you are not prepared to take this responsibility.

Bear in mind when you start that no-trump contracts are not made very often, and you should not go out of your way to look for them: if they are a possibility, they will become obvious from the progress of the bidding. During the course of the auction, however, a *bid* in no-trumps may be made several times, as it is a way of keeping the auction open while you are (both) groping towards a mutually agreeable contract.

Always open in your longest suit, even if it does not have the highest point-strength. With two suits of equal length, bid the higher valued of them first (e.g. hearts rather than diamonds). This will enable you to mention your second suit at a higher level next time you bid, while leaving the first suit available for re-bidding by yourself or your partner without having to take it to a yet higher and possibly untenable level.

More often than not your opening bid will be at the 'one' level. Circumstances in which you might open at the level of two, three or even four are set out in the following table.

In suit, a bid of one implies that you would be content with a contract to win seven in the suit if your partner should pass, but that you will make another bid if he responds to it.

Two is described as 'forcing' – it demands that your partner should not pass but name his best suit, however bad his hand. You will then come back again and take the responsibility. (Bridge players may prefer to use the two-club convention, but this is probably less appropriate to Contract Whist.)

Three is described as 'pre-emptive' or 'shut-out', since it starts the bidding at such a high level that your opponents will probably be prevented from communicating anything to each other. This is enough to compensate for the possible riskiness of the hand if your partner should pass, though with seven in your own suit the prospects are encouraging.

Four is like three, but with support of your own in side-suits.

Opening bids: what they convey to partner

Level	In a suit – your longest, or the higher of two equally long	At no-trump – should imply balanced distribution
one	I have a playable hand of 13–20 points and no suit longer than this.	I have a balanced hand of 16-18 points and no suit longer than four.
two	I have a playable hand worth about 25. Do not pass: bid your strong suit, or no trumps if none.	My balanced hand of at least 21 suggests good prospects. It is good for 2 NT if you pass, but if you have a good suit, do bid it.
three	I have at least seven cards of this suit but nothing else to speak of. Any suggestions?	I have at least 23, am safe in all suits, and would expect to win nine tricks with the minimum of support from you.
four	I have at least seven cards of this suit and would expect to win eight tricks on this hand alone.	—

A no-trump opening tells your partner that you are not worried about the contract if he leaves you in it, but if he has a good suit of his own you can either support it on the side or perhaps even join in with it.

Higher bids should be reached in good time, not opened, as they would prevent your own partner from communicating with you. This is of greater importance in Contract Whist than in Bridge, where one hand is played open.

Note that the meanings attached to these bids in the table only apply when the bid is actually opened, i.e. when it is the first bid announced between the partners. For example, a bid of three in suit does not imply a seven-card holding if any other bid has already been mentioned by either partner.

Responses. Now swap places with your partner and assume that he has made an opening bid, thus communicating the information shown in the preceding table. In order to respond, you yourself do not need a hand that would be strong enough to open the bidding with. Unless you are very weak indeed, your purpose is primarily to give him some descriptive information about your own hand. Do not refrain from mentioning a suit for fear that he will leave you in it. If he opened with a suit he is bound to re-bid, and if he opened at no-trump then he must have good support for anything you do mention.

General. With 5 points and no lengthy suit, pass, unless forced to bid by an opening bid of two in suit. With 6+ points, you can support your partner and are morally obliged to make a bid. With a hand strong enough to have opened on, make a jump-bid – that is, one at a higher level than necessary (e.g. by overcalling 1 ♠ by 3 ♣ rather than 2 ♣). This forces your partner not only to respond but to keep open the bidding until you reach a contract.

Generally, if your hand is unevenly distributed, bid in suit – your longest or strongest, or, as between equals, that of lower bidding value (e.g. diamonds rather than hearts). If it is balanced, and always if it is 4-3-3-3, respond at no-trump. This applies even if the hand is too weak for a no-trump contract. A no-trump response is often used to deny a particular suit holding rather than to assert strength in all suits, and it has the advantage of not increasing the level of the bid.

Now consider your response:

To one in suit. Respond in the same suit as your partner if you have four cards in it, or three including Ace, King or Queen.

If not, change the suit and bid your own best or cheapest ('cheap' meaning low in bidding value). If, in order to do this, you have to raise the level – for example, an opening 1 ♠ can only be followed by a bid at the 'two' level – you should have about 10 points in hand to justify the raise.

Reply 1 NT if you have some general support (6–10 points), but are weak in the suit bid and have none of your own to offer.

To one no trump. Reply at no trumps if your hand is balanced, or in your longest or strongest suit if not. With around 10 points bid two; with 15 or more jump to three.

To two in suit. You are required to bid your best suit. If you have no reasonable suit, bid 2 NT to indicate that weakness.

To two no-trump. With a balanced hand, reply at no-trump, jumping to four if particularly strong. With extreme imbalance (6+ cards in one suit, one or a void in another), reply in suit.

To higher opening bids. Play it by ear.

Re-bids. When you come to re-bid you cannot rely on tables but must be guided by what you can see and hear – and *over*hear. Until you gain experience, fight shy of jump-raises but continue to approach your contract step by step. Do not, however, fight shy of testing other suits by bidding them without seriously proposing them as trumps. This all forms part of the process of communication. Even what you and your partner do *not* mention is significant.

If you both mention the same suit, it will probably turn out to be your final contract. If you each stick to a single – but different – suit, you may have to admit to a misfit and pull out. A misfit occurs when you each have one very strong suit, but not the same one, and are both weak in the unmentioned suits. If your partner mentions a third suit, do not pass and leave him with it. He may well be feeling for a no-trump contract, so either respond at no-trump or in the fourth suit if it seems feasible, or else repeat a previously-mentioned suit.

Defensive bidding. This is what you undertake when you open the bidding for your partnership after the opponents have opened the auction – typically, when you are sitting to the dealer's left and he has made an opening bid. This puts you in quite a different position, since strength has already been declared against you and you have a certain amount of information about your opponents' possibilities.

Assuming he has opened one in suit, the first thing *not* to do is to get over-excited if you find yourself with apparent strength in the same suit. The principles on which you do act are equally valid whether you are strong or weak in it. Look instead for strength in your own hand. With a good suit you may simply overcall the opener's bid with a higher one. With strength in all suits but none that immediately jumps out at you, you *may* bid 1 NT but are much better served by doubling, for reasons explained below.

Overbidding. The hand most suitable for overcalling is one of a different shape from that needed for opening. Paradoxically, you do not need a high point count to justify overbidding – a minimum of ten may be sufficient. What you do need is a long suit, of at least five cards. In return, your partner should respond if he has 8 points for strength and can see at least three tricks in the suit you propose.

With a very strong hand – such as a count of 13 and a suit of at least six cards – you may jump your initial overbid to the 'two' level. With seven in the suit, at least consider the idea of starting at three and shutting your opponents out.

Doubling. With no outstanding suit, but general strength, you can adopt the handy device of the *informatory double* or 'take-out' double (not to be confused with a double-take, though it might give rise to one). The fact that you double does not imply to your partner that you yourself are strong in the suit quoted: it merely saves you the trouble of being forced into a higher bid (such as 1 NT), and tells him that you lack a notably biddable suit of your own but have sufficient strength to support any suit that he might care to name. Indeed, your double calls upon him to name a suit instead of passing. For this reason you must be sure to have at least one suit of your own to fall back on if his suggestion proves to be the one you were least hoping to hear.

The cue bid. You might have the sort of hand on which, as first to speak, you would have opened with a forcing bid of two or even three. In this circumstance you could draw on another Bridge convention called the 'cue bid'. To effect it, you overcall the opener's bid of one in suit by bidding two in the *same* suit, regardless of your holding in it. You may even be void; that doesn't matter. This bid is forcing: it tells your partner to keep the bidding open until you have reached a contract and guarantees that you will come back with a re-bid. He for his part must respond by naming his longest suit.

Be warned that the cue bid can land you in hot water if you are not careful. Use it only if you are convinced that it is the best line to take in the circumstances and that you are confident of making something out of whatever your partner responds. And, since it is a convention and not a logical bid with an obvious meaning, make sure that you are playing with a partner who knows all about it!

Defending against one no-trump. To overbid an opening of 1 NT with two of a suit or 2 NT, it is obvious that you need sufficient strength to cover any eventuality. The bid may also be countered by doubling, which will be understood by your partner to indicate that you have sufficient high card strength in all suits genuinely to challenge the original call. He will not automatically treat it as a call to name his longest suit, but will pass if he feels that the best course is to help you defeat the opponents' contract; alternatively, he will raise to 2NT in the unlikely event that he also has high general strength, or else treat the double as informatory by naming his longest suit, if he is long enough in it to propose a serious contract (six cards at least); but he will be relying on you to provide the side-suit support.

Penalty doubles. Let us be quite clear about the circumstances in which doubling is informatory, i.e. asks for partner's longest suit, as opposed to ordinary or 'penalty' doubles made in the belief that one can defeat the opponents' contract and so score a whopping bonus.

The following are penalty doubles:

1. Any double made when partner has already made a bid.
2. Any double of two (or more) no trumps, or three (or more) in suit.

Card play. It is in the play of the cards that Contract Whist ceases to resemble Bridge and becomes more akin to classical partnership Whist, so at this point experience of the latter will serve you in better stead than knowledge of the former.

The highly detailed opening lead conventions of Whist, though applicable to Contract Whist, are less vital here, since the process of bidding will have produced a certain amount of information as to the lie of the cards and the distribution of suits. You may therefore start by attacking in suits known to be weak in your opponents' hands or strong in your own.

Equally applicable are such principles as winning tricks as cheaply as possible, playing the lowest card of a sequence, and playing, from a suit in which you hold but two cards, high before low to indicate a void and a call for trumps. The lead of the fourth best from a weak suit enables you to employ the 'rule of eleven' to assist in the drawing of further inferences (see page 14).

The contracting partnership must always bear in mind that good play may sometimes save a shaky contract, but bad play will lose *any* contract, whether sound or not.

Sample game. South deals as follows:

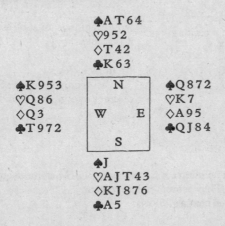

```
                    ♠ A T 6 4
                    ♡ 9 5 2
                    ◇ T 4 2
                    ♣ K 6 3
    ♠ K 9 5 3        ┌─────────┐        ♠ Q 8 7 2
    ♡ Q 8 6          │    N    │        ♡ K 7
    ◇ Q 3            │ W     E │        ◇ A 9 5
    ♣ T 9 7 2        │    S    │        ♣ Q J 8 4
                    └─────────┘
                    ♠ J
                    ♡ A J T 4 3
                    ◇ K J 8 7 6
                    ♣ A 5
```

South	West	North	East
1 ♡	no	1 NT	no
2 ◇	no	2 ♡	no . . . and all pass.

South opened with the senior of his two five-card holdings in a strong hand worth 17 points. North's bid indicates enough support to entertain another suggestion, but nothing biddable himself. South then names his other suit, diamonds. This is good news to North, who now knows that South is strong in the suits he himself is weak in, while he (North) can support the other two. Having himself no preference for diamonds or hearts, he nominates hearts again as being South's preferred suit.

West leads.

S	W	N	E	
♣ A	♣ T	♣ 3	♣ 8	
♠ J	♠ K	♠ A	♠ 2	S invites N to lead hearts.
♡ 3	♡ Q	♡ 9	♡ 7	Now that the Queen is out, S may be able to finesse against the King.
♣ 5	♣ 9	♣ K	♣ 4	Having put N back in again, the finesse can work:
♡ A	♡ 6	♡ 5	♡ K	The King is forced out, and S-N have established the trump suit.
♡ J	♡ 6	♡ 2	♠ 7	
◇ K	◇ 3	◇ 2	◇ A	Now diamonds must be established if possible.
♡ 4	♣ 2	♣ 6	♣ Q	
◇ J	◇ Q	◇ 4	◇ 5	An unlucky lead.
♡ T	♣ 7	♣ 4	♣ J	The last trump is drawn; S cannot re-enter to establish diamonds.
◇ 6	♠ 3	◇ T	◇ 9	
◇ 7	♠ 5	♠ T	♠ Q	
◇ 8	♠ 9	♠ 6	♠ 8	

Result: The contract is just made, N-S having taken the two odd tricks. They score 6 points to game.

West deals next as follows:

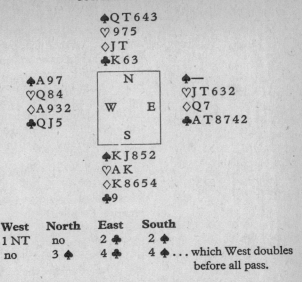

```
                    ♠Q T 6 4 3
                    ♡9 7 5
                    ◊J T
                    ♣K 6 3
    ♠A 9 7              N              ♠—
    ♡Q 8 4                             ♡J T 6 3 2
    ◊A 9 3 2         W     E           ◊Q 7
    ♣Q J 5                             ♣A T 8 7 4 2
                        S
                    ♠K J 8 5 2
                    ♡A K
                    ◊K 8 6 5 4
                    ♣9
```

West	North	East	South
1 NT	no	2 ♣	2 ♠
no	3 ♠	4 ♣	4 ♠ . . . which West doubles
			before all pass.

West bids support on the strength of a balanced hand, to
which East responds with an imbalance towards clubs. Their
conversation is interrupted by South, who overbids with the
stronger of his two suits, and North, who indicates his length in
the suit by raising the level. East re-asserts his long suit, which
South overcalls on the strength of his partner's raise in the same
suit. West's double is based on his reasonable estimate that careful play will produce the five tricks needed to beat the contract.

S	W	N	E	
♠ 2	♠ A	♠ 3	♡ 2	W leads the Ace to weaken the opponents' trumps: since they have five each, the only good use they can make of them is to cross-ruff – i.e., create a void in each hand and then alternately lead into the other's, so that the trumps will win individually by ruffing instead of falling two at a time to the same trick.
♠ 8	♠ 7	♠ 4	♣ 2	W draws another two for his one.
♡ A	♡ 4	♡ 5	♡ 3	
♢ K	♢ 8	♡ 7	♡ 6	S has created one of the voids and now puts his partner in:
♠ 5	♠ 9	♠ T	♣ 4	
♢ K	♢ A	♢ J	♢ Q	But West takes over ...
♣ 9	♣ Q	♣ K	♣ A	... and leads into East's clubs for the fourth of the five they are after.
♠ J	♣ 5	♣ 3	♣ T	Only three trumps left in play: East's clubs may yet be permitted another trick.
♢ 4	♢ 7	♢ 8	♢ 2	
♣ K	♡ Q	♡ 9	♡ T	N crosses to S, as originally envisaged by W, and S must play his last trump.
♢ 8	♢ 9	♠ 6	♣ 7	S crosses back ...
♢ 5	♢ 3	♠ Q	♡ J	N leads his last trump ...
♢ 6	♣ J	♠ 6	♣ 8	... and is obliged to lead straight into the arms (clubs) of E-W.

Result: N-S are down one trick, doubled, on their contract, giving their opponents a bonus of 20. The contract was defeated through West's foresight, which he was able to put into immediate effect by virtue of his leading position. A particularly instructive deal, and well worth studying.

North deals the third hand:

```
              ♠962
              ♡AJ9542
              ◇J8
              ♣93
♠KQ85      ┌───────────┐   ♠T743
♡KQ        │     N     │   ♡T863
◇953       │  W     E  │   ◇T2
♣T654      │     S     │   ♣QJ8
           └───────────┘
              ♠AJ
              ♡7
              ◇AKQ764
              ♣AK72
```

North	East	South	West
no	no	2 ◇	no
2 ♡	no	3 ◇	no
3 NT	no	4 ◇	no . . . and all pass.

Holding North's cards, the beginner might be carried away by
the length of the heart suit. But it is worth only 7 points, and
an opening bid of 'one' must be taken to imply at least 13. Therefore North is correct to pass, as he can always come back in if
circumstances warrant.

South, therefore, finds himself in the opening position, and
bids at the 'two' level to demand that his partner declare his best
suit. North duly replies in hearts, which is exactly what South
was looking for. South raises to three, and stays in diamonds at
the four level after North's no-trump interpolation denies
support in side-suits.

West leads.

S	W	N	E	
♠A	♠K	♠2	♠3	Conventional lead by W (see 'opening leads' at Whist), after which it is clear he has the Queen.
♣K	♣4	♣9	♣8	S apparently tests clubs on the off-chance that his partner is void.
♣A	♣5	♣3	♣J	Which he now is, having played high-low to show the clearance of his doubleton.
♣2	♣6	◇8	♣Q	
◇Q	◇3	◇J	◇2	S overtakes his partner's winning Jack in order to get the lead and put into operation a plan to 'squeeze' the top honours out of E–W's possession.
◇K	◇5	♡9	◇T	The first step is to draw out adverse trumps.
◇A	D 9	♡2	♠4	
◇7	♠5	♠6	♡3	Step two is to force discards that will strip the King and Queens (♠ and ♡) of their support.
◇6	♠8	♠9	♡6	After this, West has left only ♠Q ♡K ♡Q ♣T.
◇4	♣T	♡4	♠7	
♣9	♠Q	♡5	♡8	The first Queen falls . . .
♠J	♡Q	♡J	♠T	and the second . . .
♡7	♡K	♡A	♡T	and the King to the Ace.

Result: N–S take all thirteen tricks for a game score of 12 (4 ◇) and 6 above the line for three overtricks.

EUCHRE
A game of bowers

Euchre is the major representative of a group of trick-and-trump games in which only five cards are dealt and five tricks played, the object being to win the majority (three or more) and preferably the lot, the latter feat being termed 'winning a march' – or perhaps stealing it ? Other five-card games include Ecarte, Nap and Five Hundred.

Euchre is an American game of German-immigrant origin dating from about the 1860s. Specifically, it is traced to the so-called Dutch of Pennsylvania (Dutch = Deutsch = German in this case), and is played mainly in the north-eastern states as well as in Canada. For some curious reason it is also the usual pub-game of Britain's West country, in defiance of the otherwise universal preference for Cribbage. There is, however, no evidence to suggest that it originated in Britain and travelled westwards over the Atlantic rather than vice versa.

There are versions of Euchre for different numbers of players, and variant forms even of those versions, it being a highly prolific and cross-bred family of games. Partnership Euchre, as described below, may be regarded as a, if not *the*, classic form of the game, though two-hand Euchre probably preceded it.

A characteristic feature of Euchre games is the peculiarity of the trump suit. The highest trump is always the Jack, which is called the 'right bower'. This is followed by the other Jack of the same colour as the first, called the 'left bower'. The Ace comes next, being third highest, and so on downwards. Bower rhymes with 'flower'; it comes from the German word *Bauer* which primarily means 'farmer' (as do the related Dutch word *boer* and its English derivative *boor*), but is also one of several words for the Jack or Knave at cards.

The effect of the bowers is to lengthen the trump suit and correspondingly shorten the others, especially the suit of the same colour. Since the game is played with a 32-card pack, only eight in each suit, the numerical imbalance is of some significance to the play. Euchre is a fast game and much fun, but it is also one of deadly subtlety, as you will discover to your cost if you play against an expert. And especially if you are foolish enough to play for money.

The game

Cards. 32, consisting of the A K Q J T 9 8 7 of each suit; lower cards are customarily used for marking the score, as shown in Fig. 3.

Preliminaries. Determine partnerships by drawing cards. Ace counts low (below Seven); the two drawing the lowest cards play the two drawing the highest, and partners sit opposite each other. The player who drew the lowest card deals first. All play proceeds clockwise, including the turn to deal. Game is usually set at five points, though seven and ten are common alternatives.

Shuffle and deal. Anyone may shuffle, but dealer has the right to shuffle last. Deal five cards to each player, not singly but in batches – either two then three, or three then two (but, whichever is adopted, the same for everybody). Place the remaining cards face down to one side of the table, and turn up the top card. The suit of this card is the prospective trump suit, though it may be rejected in favour of another later.

Rank of cards. The normal rank of cards for trick-taking purposes is A K Q J T 9 8 7, but trumps are peculiar. The highest trump is the Jack of trumps, called the right bower; second highest is the other Jack of the same colour as trumps, called the left bower. Ace is therefore the third highest trump, and so downwards. It is important to understand that the left bower belongs to the trump suit and *not* to the suit shown on its face.

Dealer's privilege. If the suit of the turn-up is in fact accepted as trump, dealer is entitled to take the turn-up into his own hand and discard any other card face down in its place. Knowledge of this fact may influence the bidding.

Bidding. The player left of dealer is called eldest; the others may be referred to as secondhand, thirdhand and dealer. Starting with eldest, each in turn passes or accepts the suit of the turn-up as trumps. Whoever accepts the prospective trump is called the maker, and his partnership is thereby obliged to win three or more tricks.

As a matter of tradition, an opponent of the dealer (eldest or thirdhand) signifies his acceptance of the trump by saying 'I order it up' – meaning, in effect, that he is ordering the dealer to take up the turned card. Secondhand accepts by saying 'I assist', meaning that he will assist the dealer to win after the latter has taken the turn-up. Dealer accepts by saying 'I take it up'.

If the first three players pass, and dealer also refuses to accept the trump, he announces 'I turn it down', thereupon taking the turn-up and replacing it (still face up) crosswise at the bottom of the undealt cards so that it is still visible.

In this event there is another round of bidding, starting with eldest, in which each player in turn may either pass again or nominate a different suit as trump. (The suit that has already been rejected may not be nominated a second time.)

If all players pass a second time, the round is abandoned and the deal passes to the left.

As soon as any player has made a positive bid, either by accepting the turned up trump or by nominating another on the second round, the bidding ends and the play begins.

Playing alone. The maker is entitled to play alone against his opponents, which he signifies by stating 'alone' as soon as he has accepted or nominated the trump suit. His partner thereupon lays his cards face down on the table and does not participate in the play. The main advantage of going it alone is that the player scores double for his side if he succeeds in winning a march (all five tricks).

If the maker elects to play alone, either opponent may say 'I defend alone', in which case his partner also lays his cards face down and does not participate.

The play. Eldest leads to the first trick regardless of who is the maker, unless the maker is playing alone, in which case the lead is made by the player at maker's left. The usual rules of trick-taking apply: follow suit to the card led if possible; if not, either trump or discard. The trick is won by the highest card of the suit led, or by the highest trump if any are played. The winner of a trick leads to the next. Remember that the left bower is not a card of the suit marked on its face but is the second highest card of the trump suit.

Scoring. If the making side wins three or four tricks it scores one, whether the game was played in partnership or alone.

If the making side wins the march it scores 2 if played in partnership, 4 if played alone.

If the making side fails to win three tricks it is 'euchred'. The opposing side score 2 if it played in partnership, 4 if defended alone.

Hints on play

Here are the basic facts of Euchre life, which you must bear in mind before you start the game.

Fewer than two thirds of the cards are in play, which means that the assessment of your own hand must be made on the probability that certain key cards – such as the right bower, if you hold the left – are actually in play. Although the distribution of cards is a matter of pure chance, one's judgment of play against the probabilities is a matter of skill and experience. Players who come to Euchre from games in which all cards are dealt, such as Whist and Bridge, may be tempted to underestimate the extent to which experts can play successfully *with* the probabilities rather than *against* them.

The peculiar ranking of Jacks must be borne in mind when assessing your hand. Suppose, for example, you hold ♠7 ♡J 7 ♣— ◇J 7. If the turn-up is a black card your hand is useless. If red, however, then both your Jacks are bowers and one of the Sevens a trump, giving you a certain two and a highly probable three, even without your partner's assistance. Naturally, you will lose no opportunity to entrump a red suit.

With only five cards in hand it is unlikely that a plain suit will

FIGURE 3

Traditional method of score-keeping involves lower cards (Three and Four) not used in actual play. The Three is half-covered to denote a score of '1', the Four half-covered to denote '2', then both respectively uncovered to show '3' and '4'.

go round twice without being trumped. In your original hand, then, a plain suit void is strong because you might be able to trump it, and a one- or two-card suit strong if headed by Ace or even King. Anything longer is likely to be trumped early.

It is, however, often possible to establish a plain suit, and the early drawing of trumps for this purpose is a common strategy. Holding, for example, ♡J, ◇J, ♠A Q 7, with hearts trump, you can reasonably expect to draw all adverse trumps by leading the Jacks and then hope to win all three spades. This would not be 'best' play from the hand quoted, but could be indulged in as an emergency lone hand for a possible four points when your opponents stand at four and your own side at one.

As a general rule, if you have two certain tricks you can expect your partner to contribute a third in order to justify your becoming the maker.

Bidding. Now consider the first round of bidding for acceptance or rejection of the turn-up from each player's point of view.

As eldest, you have no indication of your partner's strength and dealer has an advantage over you by virtue of his privilege of taking the trump turn-up, the rank of which you must take very much into account. In these circumstances you need a secure trump holding to justify a bid, such as one of the bowers and two good trumps. Since you have the lead (except, possibly, against a lone player), a plain suit Ace may be counted as a reliable trick if your holding is not too long.

As secondhand, it is your partner who has the privilege of the turn-up, and you may reasonably bid on the strength of two good trumps or two otherwise reliable tricks.

As thirdhand, your partner must have indicated weakness by his pass; if you bid, the onus will be upon you, and it will be difficult to exercise by virtue of the fact that your partner, as eldest, will have the lead against you. You must therefore have two certain tricks before you may order it up. If you have a good three or more tricks, it may be worth playing alone.

As dealer, three preceding passes will put you in a good position to take it up, though your partner's admitted weakness requires you to be sure of two tricks yourself. Bear in mind that if you turn it down it is your opponents who will have the first opportunity of nominating an alternative trump, for which reason you may be justified in bidding on a risky hand in order to obviate the danger of their winning a march, especially if played alone. Here you may 'play to the score' – a procedure that applies to every player but to dealer most of all. At 0–0 you have little to lose and something to gain from taking the chance, but at 4–2 in your favour you have everything to gain and hardly anything to lose.

If everybody passes, the bidding goes round again, this time for another suit.

As eldest, look first at the possibility of entrumping the other suit of the same colour as the original turn-up (called 'making it next'), since the fact that dealer's side passed first implies that neither of them held a bower.

As secondhand, you will prefer if possible to nominate a suit of the other colour (called 'crossing it') for the same reason that eldest would have preferred to make it next.

As thirdhand, you would also prefer to make it next, but this time warily, since your partner has admitted himself weak.

Dealer, of course, would prefer to cross it, but with the same reservations.

Playing to the score. When the score stands at 0–0, you should only order it up as an opponent of the dealer's side (that is, as eldest or thirdhand) if you are certain of a win and have no alternative suit to nominate, for if all players pass you will have the first opportunity to change suit in addition to the advantage of the lead. Dealer, on the other hand, should take it up at all costs, in order to deprive eldest of the advantage outlined above. The worst outcome of doing so would be to be euchred for a score of 2–0 against, whereas to leave it to the other side might be to invite a lone march resulting in 4–0 against.

If your opponents stand at three points and you are thirdhand or dealer, it is dangerous to become the maker in view of your partner's admitted weakness, coupled with the fact that to be euchred would lose you the game.

A side standing at four points is said to be 'at the bridge'. If you are at the bridge as dealer, and your opponents have less than three, you should take it up even on a poor hand in order to reduce the risk of a lone march from eldest.

Discarding. As a matter of form, dealer should make his discard before the first trick is led but leave the turn-up on top of the pack until he wishes to play it. (It should go without saying that the dealer's exchange privilege applies only when the suit of the turn-up is accepted; when another trump is nominated, there is nothing to exchange.)

There is no problem as to the discard – the best to throw is a plain suit singleton lower than the Ace. With a good alternative, however, a singleton King may be retained, as there is only a 62 per cent probability that the Ace is in play at all and only a 41 per cent probability that it is held by one of the opponents. The chances are therefore better than evens that the King will make a trick. Of two singletons, of course, discard the lower, and if both are of equal rank, discard preferably one of a different colour from trumps.

Playing alone. The chief attraction of playing alone is the possibility of winning a march and scoring four instead of two – indeed, there is little point in going it alone otherwise, unless, as thirdhand or dealer, you feel that your partner is so weak that his participation in the play could be less of a help than a hindrance. One advantage that accrues from playing alone is that the lead is made by the player on your left, thus putting you in the position of playing last to the first trick. It is an advantage that particularly benefits thirdhand, as the worst trick-playing position of all is lying third to the lead from a weak partner. To the dealer, however, it makes no difference, as eldest would lead anyway.

The purpose of defending alone – which may only be undertaken when the maker is playing alone – is to increase your partnership's score in the event of your euchring him. Naturally, you will only undertake a lone defence if you have a particularly strong hand.

(In some circles, only the maker may play alone, and there is no provision for either of his opponents to defend alone. In this case the lone player, if euchred, should lose double in order to penalise a rash attempt made at playing to the score – in other words, his opponents score four instead of two, as he would have done if he had won a march.)

The play. Normal practice is to lead trumps for the purpose of extracting them all round and so establishing a plain suit in which you hold the Ace and more, or (hopefully, bearing in mind the 59 per cent probability) King high. If, however, you have no qualifying plain suit, and are not particularly rich in trumps, it is better to retain what trumps you do hold for the purpose of trumping when void in suits led.

We have already observed that a plain suit is unlikely to go round twice, so there is no point in seeking a finesse. Lead your highest card, especially if it is an Ace or King, at your earliest opportunity, and, when following to the trick, win it if you can unless your partner has already done so. Remember that the trump suit is marginally longer than the others, and that an opponent is as likely to hold three trumps as to be void in them.

Sample game

You are lying thirdhand; the turn-up is ♣Q and your hand is as follows:

    ♣ K
    ◊ T 9 7
    ♠ A
    ♡ —

Not very promising. Your partner passes, and so does second-hand. Your own pass follows as a matter of course. Dealer, you are relieved to hear, turns it down, leaving it to your partner, as eldest, to nominate a suit. But again he passes, indicating considerable weakness, and so does secondhand.

This places you in an interesting spot, as the hints on play advise you not to attempt a game in diamonds; the temptation to do so is great, even though you would be crossing the suit instead of making it same. Your Ace is a sure trick, your King a 41 per cent probable trick (especially since neither opponent accepted clubs as trumps, rendering it conceivable that neither holds the Ace), and your void a very probable trick by virtue of one of your trumps – which, although fearfully low in rank, are reasonably high in length.

It is true that your partner is weak; but on the other hand so are your opponents, and you have twice as many of them, so they must be twice as weak. Convinced by this convoluted logic, and standing at the start of a new game, you nominate diamonds – but do not invite your partner to drop out.

Trick 1

Partner leads ♣J, secondhand plays ♣T, and you play your King. It all hinges on dealer. He plays ♠7. Extraordinary! He is void in both clubs (no wonder he passed first time round) and trumps; and very probably, had you passed the second time, he would have nominated hearts or spades as a sure-fire trump game.

Trick 2

You now hold a plain Ace, ♠A, and your three low trumps, T 9 7. You could surely lead the Ace with success, in view of dealer's void in trumps, and would probably then come back after leading and losing a trump for three or possibly four tricks. But if your right-hand opponent has a good trump at all it would be safer to extract it from him first. So, in the hope that your partner has one good overtaking diamond, you lead ◇T. Dealer throws ♠9, partner ◇A. Where are the bowers? Surely it will be taken? But no; your right-hand opponent plays ◇Q, thus leaving the ball in your partner's court.

Trick 3

He leads ♡7, and secondhand plays ♡Q. You trump with the Seven, and dealer throws ♡8. This leaves you with ◇9 and ♠A.

Trick 4

You lead ♠A. Not the trump – for all you know, your partner may hold the King and lead a wrong suit to the advantage of secondhand, whereas if the latter is void in diamonds you will win the march. Dealer plays ♡K, partner ♠T, followed by ♠8. Very promising.

Trick 4
Your ◊9 is followed by ♡A, ♡9, ♠J. You have four tricks and your partner one, giving you the march for two points. Here are the original hands:

```
Dealer    ♣—   ◊—   ♠9 7   ♡A K 8
Partner   ♣J   ◊A   ♠T    ♡9 7
2ndhand   ♣T   ◊Q   ♠J 8  ♡Q
```

With clubs as the prospective trump, no-one was in a position to take it or order it up, although, with hindsight, your partner could conceivably have made his Ace and right bower together with your Ace for three tricks.

On the second round he had nothing to bid, and no more did secondhand; but, as you surmised from the play, dealer might happily have made game in hearts, probably to the tune of four tricks.

A lone game. The turned up card is ♠Q and the lie of the cards as follows:

```
Eldest    ♠—   ♡K T 8   ♣Q    ◊7        passes
2ndhand   ♠—   ♡Q       ♣9    ◊A Q 9    passes
3rdhand   ♠K   ♡9       ◊Q    ♣K J      passes
Dealer    ♠J 9 ♡A 7     ♣A              takes it up.
```

Thirdhand held the King of prospective trumps (spades) and the left bower (♣J), but with nothing good in hand he correctly refrained from following his partner's pass with a bid.

Dealer can count ♠Q as part of his hand, rejecting ♡7 from the outset, and with the right bower and two good Aces decides to go it alone, as there is a fair chance of winning the march. Secondhand accordingly lays his cards down.

Eldest leads, and the play proceeds:

Eld.	2nd.	3rd.	Del.	
♡ K		♡ 9	♡ A	Having no defence against a possible march, eldest leads his only good card immediately.
◇ 7		♠ K	♠ J	Dealer can only be beaten by a guarded left bower, and plays into the situation at once.
♡ 8		♣ J	♠ Q	Enter the bower, thirdhand having thrown its guard to the previous trick. So much for the march.
♣ Q		♣ K	♠ A	
♡ T		◇ Q	♠ 9	
0		1	4	tricks, scoring 1 to dealer's partnership

Secondhand had, in fact, nothing useful to contribute to the play, and dealer was right to go it alone. He had a good chance of the march, which was beaten only by the holding of a guarded left bower in one opponent's hand. Which goes to show that a guarded left bower is a good defence to an opponent's solo march.

4

This is the simplest of the Jass games (pronounced *yass*), which as a family are played extensively throughout Europe though thought to be of Dutch origin. They include such games as Klaberjass or Kalabriasz, Pandour, and Belote. In all of them, the object is to take tricks not for their own sake but for the purpose of capturing certain scoring cards played to them, so that the winning player or side is not necessarily the one with most tricks but the one whose tricks contain the greatest total in point or 'pip' value. Scores are also made for combinations, such as sequences and four of a kind.

The most characteristic feature of Jass games is that the top card in play is the Jack of trumps, which is the Jass itself and counts 20; it is usually followed by the Nine of trumps, called Nel (or something similar in various languages), which is worth 14 to the player who captures it.

Jass games may seem forbidding at first sight to players brought up in the tradition of Whist and its relatives, where the object is simply to take tricks regardless of the cards they contain, but they are nevertheless well worth delving into. One of the most complex is also one of the best – I refer to Pandour, which is the Jass equivalent of Solo Whist. For introductory purposes, however, it will be as well to start with Klaverjass, which is the most straightforward of them all.

Jass, by the way, is one of many Germanic words for Jack, and *klaver* is the Dutch for 'clover' and 'club (suit)'; so *Klaverjass* literally means 'Jack of clubs'. Perhaps in an earlier form of the game ♣J was always highest regardless of trump suit, as it still is in the German game of Skat.

Klaverjass is about the most popular four-hand card game in the Netherlands, and – as so often happens with popular games – there are apt to be local variations in the rules of play. There is no authoritative 'standard' form, but the one presented below has been abstracted from half a dozen different Dutch sources and may therefore be regarded as at least authentic.

The game

Cards. 32, a short pack comprising A K Q J T 9 8 7 of four suits; a 'second pack' is desirable for the purpose of turning up a trump card, but of course the easiest thing to do is to use the 'other half' (Twos to Sixes) of the shortened pack for this purpose.

Game. Game is usually 1500 up, which takes several deals, and as points are being scored constantly it is convenient to use some sort of mechanical marker or a Cribbage board to record them.

Deal. Deal a batch of four cards to each player, then another batch of four, so that everyone has eight cards. Shuffle the second pack and turn up the top card to establish trumps.

General idea. There is a round of bidding, as the result of which one partnership challenges the other to a game. In play, each side's object is to score more points for tricks and combinations than the other. The losing side scores nothing, but if the defenders beat the challengers they score far more than the challengers would have made if they had succeeded.

Rank and value of cards in tricks. For trick-taking purposes, cards rank from high to low in the following order and have face or 'pip' values as shown:

J of trumps (Jass)	20
9 of trumps (Nel)	14
Ace	11 each
Ten	10 each
King	4 each
Queen	3 each
Jack (unless trump)	2 each
Nine (unless trump)	0
Eight	0
Seven	0

Note that in non-trump suits the highest card is Ace and the second highest Ten, but in trumps Ace and Ten are only third and fourth highest respectively.

FIGURE 4
A good hand if spades are turned as the trump suit. Jack and
Nine rank as Jass and Nel, highest in their suit for an
eventual won-trick pip count of 20+14, while the King and
Queen score 20 for marriage, plus 20 for a sequence of three
with the Jack (even though, for trick-taking purposes, it ranks
highest). Not a good hand, however, if hearts are turned: Ace
is only third highest.

Note also that, in addition to these pip-values when won in
tricks, an extra 10 is scored for winning the last trick. *Thus the
total number of points to be played for in tricks is 162.*

Card combinations. The following combinations can be scored
from hand, i.e. any player holding such a combination may show
it and score it to his partnership's credit:

Four Jacks	200
Four Aces, Kings or Queens	100
Sequence of five or more	100
Sequence of four	50
Sequence of three	20
Marriage, i.e. K+Q trumps	20

A sequence is three or more cards *of the same suit* and in numerical sequence – for this purpose alone, cards rank in their traditional order of A K Q J T 9 8 7 in all suits. (Thus, for example, Q J T of trumps form a sequence of three, even though they are widely separated for trick-taking purposes.)

A card may be counted as part of more than one combination. For example, a holding of A K Q J in trumps counts 50 for the sequence plus 20 for the marriage, and any one of them may also form part of a set of four. Note that K + Q form a marriage only in the trump suit, and not in any of the other three.

Combinations may also be scored when they occur in tricks as explained later.

Bidding. Starting at left of dealer, each player has one turn to pass or 'play'. A player bids if he thinks he and his partner together will make more points for tricks and combinations than their opponents, using the turn-up suit as trumps. As soon as one player says 'play' his side becomes the challenging side.

If all players pass, player left of dealer may either choose a different trump suit, in which case he automatically makes a challenge, or pass again, in which case there is a new deal. (*Variant:* If all pass, the next card of the second pack is turned up and there is another round of bidding. If it is the same suit as the first, or if all players pass again, there is a new deal.)

Leading and scoring combinations. Player left of dealer always leads to the first trick, regardless of which was the bidding side. Any player who has a scoring combination in hand may declare and score for it at any time before a card is led to the second trick – after that it is too late. It is usual to declare a combination as you play your card to the first trick. Whoever wins the first trick should ask if anyone has anything to declare before leading to the second.

Play of tricks. The winner of each trick leads to the next. You must follow suit to the card led if possible. If not, you *must* trump, and furthermore, if someone else has already trumped, you must play a *higher* trump if you can, even if it means over-trumping your own partner. If trumps are led, each player must try to take the trick if he can. That is, you must play a trump higher than the highest one already showing, if you can.

Only if you have no card of the suit led and no trumps at all may you discard from another suit.

The trick is won by the highest card of the suit led or by the highest trump if any are played.

Combinations 'on the table'. A feature of play which is quite unique to Klaverjass is that combinations may be scored 'on the table'; this means that if the four cards played to a trick include a combination, the score for that combination is credited to the side of the player winning the trick. (For example, if Ten of trumps is led, and the other cards played are Queen, King and Jack of trumps, then the player of the Jack – which wins the trick – scores 50 for the sequence, plus 20 for the marriage, as well as the combined pip-values of the cards, which in themselves come to 37; total value of trick, 107!)

Scoring. Whoever wins the last trick scores 10 for it. Unless trick values have been noted as you go along, each partnership puts its own tricks together and sorts through the cards to calculate the total value of all pip-cards it contains. (The pip-values of the two partnerships together should total 152, plus ten for last.) Finally, each side adds in whatever it made for combinations scored from the hand or on the table. Whichever side has the greater total wins.

If the challengers win, they score what they make. If not, the defenders score what they make *plus* what the challengers make.

Hints on play

Until you get used to the game it is hard to estimate what sort of score you can expect to make in tricks and pips. All you can do is to survey your hand generally and decide whether it seems broadly strong or broadly weak. Strong points are long trumps (four or more, or three high ones), high cards (Aces and Tens) in short side-suits, and voids, which will enable you to 'catch' cards of high pip value when led from that suit. Any singleton

FIGURE 5

A combination scored 'on the table'. North leads ◇T, East follows suit, South adds the Jack for a sequence of three (counting 20) on the assumption that his partner's Ten will win. West, however, is void and trumps with the Nel, gaining a trick counting 20 immediately plus $10+3+2+14 = 29$ in pips towards game. Note that the Ten counts in sequence with Jack and Queen, even though second highest in the suit for trick-taking purposes.

other than a side Ace or the top trump is a weakness, and the higher its pip value the weaker it is.

If the hand is broadly strong then you should certainly be prepared to challenge, even if you have little or nothing by way of combinations, as it is worth hoping that your partner will have something to declare. If the hand is broadly weak, however, do not automatically pass, for any score you make for high combinations will be more than useful. An extreme illustration of this point is that with all four Jacks you score 200, while the most your opponents could make in tricks and pips would be 142.

Combinations made on the table cannot be taken into account at the bidding stage, as they are rare and chancy. Not very helpful is the fact that you can immediately tell what combinations will *not* be made on the table – namely, any of which you yourself hold two or more cards.

Don't forget that in any game where cards are dealt in batches an unbalanced distribution of cards between the suits is usual rather than exceptional.

Bear in mind that any combination you declare from the hand gives valuable information as to your holding to *two* opponents but only *one* partner, as it is obligatory to identify the scoring cards (and show them if so requested). This fact should not inhibit you from declaring them, as they are likely to be worth enough to compensate for the exposure. But you should thereafter bear in mind which of your cards are known and which unknown, and, wherever there is no more profitable need to the contrary, prefer to play out a known (declared) card rather than one your opponents did not know you held.

The play for tricks is noticeably affected – especially to those more used to the laws of Whist and Bridge – by the obligation to trump when void, and to overtrump where possible. This makes it easier to draw trumps for the purpose of safeguarding the subsequent lead of high cards in side-suits: you can force out any trumps available by leading from a suit in which opponents are void, and squeeze out a higher trump by the lead of a lower. The general effect this has on a game is to make it that much easier to deduce other players' holdings at an early stage. For instance, a player who fails to overtrump clearly has no high trumps, and if you haven't either the possibilities are strictly limited. This, coupled with the fact that combinations are revealed at the out-set, often leads to a situation in which you can place everyone else's cards before you get half way through the tricks.

Selecting which card to play to a trick – when you have a choice – is complicated by three factors. First, there is the question of who is already winning or is most likely to win the trick you are currently playing to. That determines whether or not you will wish to play a card of high pip value (factor two) or one likely to lead to a combination on the table (factor three).

Playing high to a trick won by your partner – a process some-times known as 'swarming' – but worthlessly to a trick won by an opponent does not call for a great deal of subtlety. Playing with a view to combinations on the table, however, is rather more intriguing, especially because the order of cards in combinations differs from that of their trick-taking powers. For example, if you are to lead from Ace, Ten of a suit when you know your opponents are void of trumps, the Ten is a better lead than the Ace. For trick-taking purposes it is as high as the Ace, and for pip-scoring purposes the difference is negligible. But it stands a much greater chance of inducing the win of a sequence on the table, such as T 9 8 or J T 9 or Q J T – three possibilities, as opposed to the single possibility of A K Q if you lead the Ace. And don't forget the marriage. If you hold King or Queen of trumps (but not both) be on the lookout for any opportunity of marrying them in a trick won by yourself or your partner. Best of all is to lead it when you know your partner has the Jack – you then stand to make a marriage and a sequence.

Sample deal

Diamonds are trumps and the cards fall as follows:

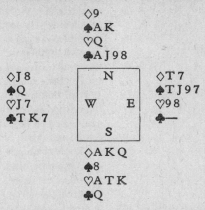

```
                    ◊9
                    ♠A K
                    ♡Q
                    ♣A J 9 8
    ◊J 8               N              ◊T 7
    ♠Q                                ♠T J 9 7
    ♡J 7          W        E          ♡9 8
    ♣T K 7                            ♣—
                       S
                    ◊A K Q
                    ♠8
                    ♡A T K
                    ♣Q
```

Three of the hands are spoilt by singleton holdings. North passes: his second-to-top trump – Nel – is particularly awkward, as he hasn't even a void to play it to. East has a useful void but nothing worth boasting about. South, however, says 'Play'.

North leads (West dealt), and East declares his sequence of three clubs for 20 before playing his card. South, before playing his, declares his trump sequence plus marriage for 40 – with the result that both North and East know that South does not have the Jass. West has nothing to declare when he plays.

We will add those scores in at the end of the game. In the following account of the play for tricks, the total value of each one – pips plus combinations on the table – is shown at the extreme left.

	N	E	S	W

7	♡ Q	♡ 8	♡ K	♡ 7	North's only way of making his Nel is to create a void and trump it later. South plays with a view to a sequence on the table – he can assume from his own holding that North was probably clearing the suit, and so leads back into it.
46	◇ 9	♡ 9	♡ T	♡ J	Just so! South leads Ten rather than Ace with a view to a sequence on the table, which actually emerges. Now everyone knows he holds Ace, the last remaining heart in play, as well as the three trumps he declared. (Note ◇ 9 = 14, sequence = 20.)
23	♣ 8	◇ T	♣ Q	♣ T	A difficult lead for North. East is obliged to trump; West swarms on it. It is now clear to all that West holds the Jass.
7	♠ K	♠ 9	♠ 8	♠ Q	East leads a known rather than unknown card …
44	♠ A	♠ T	◇ Q	◇ J	… which catches North out: he knows his partner to be void in spades (because he can place all four of South's cards), and hopes that the unknown ♠7 will lie with West. But it doesn't; and West trumps with a valuable haul. East swarms because he knows West will take it.

15	♣ A	◇ 7	◇ K	♣ 7	
11	♣ 9	♠ 7	◇ A	◇ 8	South knew he only had the Eight to catch, and with the last trump out can make with his Ace.
29	♣ J	♠ J	♡ A	♣ K	Pip value 19, plus 10 for last.
	53	23	62	44	For pips and combinations on the table, plus last.
		20	40		For combinations declared from the hand.

Thus North-South, the challenging side, wins with 155 to 87.

Footnote: A recent Dutch publication states that combinations are now widely scored 'on the table', only those in hand being ignored. It is suggested that this increases the skill factor – or at least decreases the chance factor, though the claim strikes me as debatable.

5

This pleasant little game of tricks was invented around the turn of the century by Professor Hoffman, nom-de-plume of a cards expert with several 'Hoyles' to his credit. Easy to learn and not too demanding, it introduces two quite novel features into the field of Whist-like games from which it is derived. One is the 'hier-archic' order of suits for trumping purposes, which simply means that a card of any higher suit beats one of any lower suit, regardless of rank. (Interestingly, from a historical viewpoint, the order of suits is that of the old form of Bridge. The trans-ference of spades from lowest to highest position produced the modern Bridge order, which is also to be seen in Contract Whist.)

The other novel feature is the invention of 'quints', which gives the game its name. A quint is simply a Five, or two cards of the same suit adding up to five, and it is from the making – and avoiding – of quints that the fun of the game is largely derived.

The game

Cards. 53; a standard 52-card pack plus one Joker.

Game. A rubber is won by the first side to win two games. Game is 250 up, typically reached after two or three deals. Scores may be conveniently recorded on a Cribbage board (each peg counting five) or Bézique markers.

Deal. Twelve cards each, singly; place the last five face down-wards to one side of the table to form the 'cachette'. The cachette may not be seen until the end of the round, when it is taken by the side winning the twelfth trick, and counts as a thirteenth.

Object. Points are scored for tricks in themselves, and also for certain combinations of cards – called quints – falling to a trick. Tricks are not counted until the end of the round, but quints are scored as they are taken. If a side makes game (250 points) as the result of winning a trick containing a quint, the rest of the hand is not played out.

Trumps. For trick-taking purposes, suits rank, in ascending order, spades, clubs, diamonds, hearts. A player void of the suit led can therefore trump by playing a card from any higher suit, spades being trumped by any other, clubs by any red suit, diamonds only by hearts, hearts not at all. Thus all 52 cards rank from ♠2 (lowest) up to ♡A, which cannot be beaten.

Quints. The Joker, each Five, and any two cards of the same suit totalling five in face value, are all quints. Thus a trick containing Ace and Four, or Three and Two, of the same suit scores a quint in that suit to its winner. A trick can contain more than one quint – for example, if Ace and Four of a suit fall to the same trick as any Five and the Joker, it contains three quints.

The value of quints is as follows:

Joker (Quint Royal)	25
Any quint in ♡	20
Any quint in ◇	15
Any quint in ♣	10
Any quint in ♠	5

Doubling and redoubling. After the cachette has been laid aside, but before any card is led, each in turn has one opportunity either to double, or to re-double an opponent's double. Doubling affects only the value of tricks, not of quints. Tricks are normally worth 5 each, but if doubled they count 10 each, and if re-doubled, 20 each.

Tricks. Player left of dealer leads to the first trick. Players must follow suit to the card led, except that the holder of the Joker may play it whenever he deems fit (*see below*). If unable to follow suit, a player may discard from a lower suit, or trump by playing any card of any higher suit. The trick is won by the person playing the highest card to it, bearing in mind that all cards have relatives values from ♠2 to ♡A. The winner of a

FIGURE 6

A trick rich in quints. North opens with ♠A. East must follow
suit but has only the Four, making a quint in spades for 5.
South, assuming his partner's Ace will win, plays Quint Royal
for 25. West, void in spades, trumps with a scoring card from a
higher suit, giving an additional quint in diamonds for 15. Total
quint value 45, in addition to the basic trick score.

trick scores the value of any quint it may contain, and leads to the next.

Joker. The holder of the Joker may play it at any time. It has no trick-taking value, but in its capacity as Quint Royal, worth 25, it counts to the credit of the side winning it in a trick. Its holder will therefore seek to play it to a trick being won by his partner.

(There is no official rule about leading the Joker, but the circumstance can arise in which the holder has no choice but to lead it. For this purpose I recommend that if a player leads the Joker, the player on his left determines the suit to follow.)

Last trick. Whoever takes the last (twelfth) trick takes the cachette of five cards and scores for any quint or quints it may contain. It also counts as an extra trick and scores accordingly.

Score. At the end of the round, each side adds to its score for quints a score for tricks it won, at the rate of 5 undoubled, 10 doubled or 20 re-doubled. If quints are enough to make game (250), tricks are not counted. If both sides make game on tricks, the side with the higher total wins. The first side to make two games wins the rubber, and scores an extra 100 for it.

There is no official ruling about ties, but I recommend that if both sides make equal game on tricks there should be another deal, in which case the first to score a quint is bound to win.

Hints on play

The play of Quinto is entirely shaped by the hierarchic trumping system and the value of the last trick.

The winners of the last trick win the cachette, which is worth playing for, partly for its intrinsic value as the 'odd trick' and partly for the slightly less than one-in-nine chance of its containing at least one quint. Though its average value may be small, the cachette can in certain circumstances be worth 90 to its takers – for if it contains Quint Royal (25) in a re-doubled game (20), that makes 45 to you instead of 45 to your opponents.

The surest way of winning the cachette is for the holder of the unbeatable ♡A to hold on to it until the last moment. Since you cannot be sure from the outset that your partner does not hold ♡A if you do not have it yourself, there is no point in trying to force it out early. It is, however, possible to devise some sort of signalling system whereby a player can, by his choice of lead, indicate to his partner (and his opponents) whether or not he holds the top card.

Since it is virtually impossible to establish a black suit – i.e. to force out the higher red suits in order to lead into a long run of clubs – normal procedure is to start in spades and gradually progress through the suits in ascending order, leaving hearts till last. It is sometimes possible to establish diamonds, however, if you hold the suit long and have also either length or strength in hearts for the purpose of clearing them out first.

Whoever holds the Joker will be concerned to play it to a trick won by his partner, which means that if you yourself don't hold it you must give your partner the earliest opportunity of dropping it. For this reason leader should start with ♠A if he has it, or ♣A. Only in default of black Aces or guarded Kings should ◇A be led for this purpose, and ♡A would in any case be too valuable.

The making of quints injects some interesting elements into the play. For example, when playing second to the lead of a top card you should avoid throwing anything lower than Six for fear of giving away a quint. The 2+3 quint usually happens by accident, being forced out (as in the fifth trick of the sample game given later) when its holder has no choice in the matter.

The A+4 quint can be cooperatively worked up to between the partners. You may, for example, win a trick with a King when also holding the Ace, so that with an early return in the same suit your partner may throw, or even lead, the Four if he has it. There are two common ways of making the Five quint – one, which can easily be overlooked if you are not on the ball, is to trump or overtrump with a Five when unable to follow suit. Suppose, for example, your left-hand opponent leads ♣A and your partner drops the matching Four; then your right-hand opponent, being void in clubs, might profitably trump with ◇5. If you are also void you may simply be tempted to play a higher diamond and capture both quints. But of course what you should look for is ♡5, which gives you the trick and a third quint to boot! The other way of making the Five quint is simply to drop it to a trick you know your partner can win, or is already winning.

It is obvious that a two-card quint cannot be scored if you hold both cards yourself; you can therefore safely lead one of them out, and you should be on the alert for similar play from your partner. Even more significantly, if you hold Ace and Four, circumstances may arise in which you can lead or discard the Four in order to let your partner know you have the Ace as well.

Remember that five cards are out of play, lying in the cachette, so that with an even distribution of cards there may be two or three clean tricks to be made in each suit. With a fairly even distribution, you can expect in the lower suits to make with a guarded King, but possibly not with a guarded Queen. Do not bother to lead from a lower suit when play has reached a higher one. For example, by the seventh trick the play will probably be into diamonds, so it is not worth leading a black card. Reserve the residuals of lower suits to use as discards as necessary at a later stage. This is especially important if, as the result of long black suit holdings, you have kept hold of ♣5 or ♠5. Reserve them in the hope of dropping them, when void, to tricks won by your partner. Leading them out will force everyone to trump or overtrump, and may embarrass your partner considerably.

The lower the suit, the more valuable the void. If you have no spades to start with, you are in a strong position anyway and never more so than when playing second to the trick, as your partner then has a chance to drop his Joker, or the Five quint, or the Four to an Ace lead as the case may be. Since play normally starts in spades there is no point in going out of your way to void them. With two clubs or only one, however, it is often worth clearing them out as soon as possible, even by leading them before spades. A void in diamonds is only worth having if you have plenty of hearts with which to trump them. Needless to say, a void in hearts is useless!

You should certainly double or re-double if you feel you are in a position to do so. Since the cachette counts as the odd trick, one side is bound to take more for tricks than the other, so

doubling or re-doubling increases the margin between the two
sides. In the sample deal which follows, for example, the side
that doubled finished up only 105 points off game and a good 55
in advance of their opponents. Had they not doubled, they would
have lain only 30 in advance and a good 150 points off game. The
effect is even greater in subsequent deals, where the difference
between doubling and not doubling may mean the difference
between making game on this round and losing it on the next.

To double or re-double you must be confident that your side
will take seven tricks at least, or six and the last. Reckoning your
own hand as four may not be enough if your partner can only
make two, but if you can make five (or four and last) the opportunity should be seized. Your decision will be influenced, of
course, by whether others have called or passed. Note, by the
way, that you may only re-double an opponent's double, not
your own partner's.

Sample deal

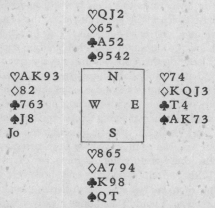

```
                    ♡Q J 2
                    ◇6 5
                    ♣A 5 2
                    ♠9 5 4 2
  ♡A K 9 3      ┌──────────┐    ♡7 4
  ◇8 2          │    N     │    ◇K Q J 3
  ♣7 6 3        │ W      E │    ♣T 4
  ♠J 8          │    S     │    ♠A K 7 3
  Jo            └──────────┘
                    ♡8 6 5
                    ◇A 7 9 4
                    ♣K 9 8
                    ♠Q T
```

West dealt. North speaks first, and declines to double. East
passes, not liking the look of his hearts, though he can probably
count on two spade tricks, a trumped club, and a diamond in its
own right. South is also unhappy with the trump situation, and
passes. West doubles: he can surely trump a spade and a

diamond, will make the two top hearts for four, and save one of them for the last trick, five. North leads.

N	E	S	W	
♣A	♣T	♣8	♣6	Possibly North's only opportunity of testing South for the Joker . . . which he has not got.
♠9	♠K	♠T	Jo	East correctly divines from the previous trick that West has it. 25 to E-W.
♠3	♠A	♠Q	♠8	
♣5	♣4	♣K	♣7	East has no further use for spades, except as discards, and now proceeds to void clubs. North duly plays the quint to his partner's win, scoring 10.
♣2	◇3	♣9	♣3	East happily trumps a two-card quint for 10. He might reasonably have taken high instead, on the off-chance of a later two-card quint in diamonds.
♠5	♠7	◇4	♠J	East throws a cat to the pigeons, having a weak heart and preferring not to lead diamonds. South, by playing the Four, indicates to his partner that he also has the matching red Ace.
◇6	◇J	◇9	◇2	
♠4	♠3	◇7	◇8	An amusing lead, but South refuses to relinquish his Ace.
♡J	♡7	♡5	♡9	South gives his partner a quint worth 20.
◇5	◇Q	◇A	♡3!	A good lead of a quint into a partner's known Ace, but unhappily trumped at the last minute.
♡2	♡4	♡6	♡A	Just by chance, another lovely quint.
♡Q	◇K	♡8	♡K	And the last trick.

The cachette contains nothing of value ($\heartsuit$T $\diamondsuit$T $\clubsuit$Q $\clubsuit$J $\spadesuit$6), but gives East-West their ninth trick, well justifying West's double. Thus the scores are:

N-S	E-W	
40	90	for tricks (doubled, 10 each)
50	55	for quints
90	145	total

Canasta is the game you graduate to when you already know one of the basic members of the Rummy family, such as that described on page 161. It is, frankly, about the most complex of all the Rummy games. But not without reason. Few Rummies provide much scope for the exercise of creative skill against the luck of the draw, most of them giving rise to a succession of game positions from which there is always a best move, with no great experience required to determine it. Canasta, however, succeeds in increasing the skill factor by confronting you with a greater variety of options and alternatives, and it is for this reason that alone of the Rummy games it has attracted the attention of serious card players all over the world. It has also given rise to yet more complex derivatives such as Samba, Bolivia and others, but they need not detain us here. Complexity in itself is not a desirable property of card games, and can all too easily be overdone.

Canasta originated in Uruguay during the 1940s. The word itself is Spanish for 'basket', and denotes the high-scoring combination consisting of seven cards of the same rank. Ely Culbertson,* the man who virtually invented Bridge as we know it, explains the image thus:

> The Spanish word for 'weaving' is *tejiendo*. *Tejiendo las cartas*, that is, 'weaving the cards', is a colourful Spanish way of saying that a meld of three of a kind, or more, is being 'woven' together. And when the biggest meld of all, the canasta, is completed, you naturally have woven a 'basket'.
>
> *Culbertson on Canasta*, Faber, 1950

So – let's get weaving.

---

* Culbertson on Canasta, Faber & Faber, 1950.

The game

Cards. 108, consisting of two standard 52-card packs with four Jokers. They need not all be of the same back design and colour, but must be of the same size.

Game. Partners sit opposite each other, North-South versus East-West. A game may consist of one or more deals and is won by the first side to reach or exceed 5000 points. If both sides reach it on the same deal the one with the higher total wins. Scores are recorded at the end of each deal.

Deal. Decide first dealer by any agreed means; thereafter the turn to deal passes to the left. Deal eleven cards each, in ones. Place the undealt cards face down and squared up in the middle of the table to form the *stock*. Turn up the top card of the stock and lay it face up beside the stock. This starts the discard pile – best referred to as the *pack* – which must also be kept squared up throughout the game. The card on top of the pack is known as the upcard. If the first upcard is a Joker, a Two or a red Three, it must immediately be covered by the next card of the stock, and so on until the upcard is of some other rank or a black Three.

With the stock and the first upcard settled, any player who has been dealt a red Three must place it face up on the table before him and is then dealt the top card of the stock to bring his hand back to eleven cards.

You are now ready to start play, but should first note the following basic facts about the game, which will give you an initial sense of direction.

General information. The object of the game is to collect and display on the table batches of three or more cards of the same rank, such batches being called melds. A meld of seven or more cards is a canasta, and no-one can end the game until his side has made at least one of them.

Jokers and Twos are 'wild' cards: they cannot be melded but can form part of melds based on 'natural' cards by themselves (i.e. ranks from Four up to Ace). Threes have special powers, as outlined below.

All meldable cards have a melding value, which at the end of the game counts to your credit if they are out in melds, but against you if still left in hand. The set values are:

Jokers	50 each
Aces and Twos	20 each
High cards (K Q J T 9 8)	10 each
Low cards (7 6 5 4 and black 3)	5 each

In addition to the melding value of individual cards, each completed canasta carries a bonus of 500 if it consists entirely of natural cards, 300 if it contains one or more wild cards. (These are known respectively as a 'natural' and a 'mixed' canasta.)

Black Threes may only be melded when you are 'going out', as explained later.

Red Threes are bonus cards. Every time you get one you must lay it face up on the table before you. They are worth 100 each (doubled if you get all four) and count in your favour if you have made any melds, but against you if you have not.

The game normally ends when one player 'goes out' by melding in one turn all the cards left in his hand.

Finally, you must be aware that Canasta is essentially a partnership game. Partners keep melds made by both of them together in one place on the table, not separately in front of each. And it is sometimes inadvisable to end the game by going out without first asking your partner's permission.

General procedure. Starting with the person at dealer's left, each player in turn does one or more of three things in the following order:

1. Draw (top card of stock, or discard pile if permitted)
2. Meld (if any possible, and subject to certain restrictions)
3. Discard (unless gone out by melding all cards left in hand).

Draw: You may always take the top card of the stock and add it to your hand. If you draw a red Three, you place it face up before you and draw again.

Instead of drawing from stock, you may take the whole of the pack, provided that you can immediately meld the upcard – either by adding it to one of your existing melds on the table, or by using it to start a new meld in conjunction with two or more matching cards from your own hand (for which purpose a matching natural card plus one wild card is sufficient, though some insist that you must hold a natural pair to start a new meld with the upcard).

But you may not take the discard pile in this way if it is *frozen*, which it is in the following circumstances:

1. It is frozen to you and your partner until your side has made its first meld.
2. It is frozen to everybody whenever it contains a wild card (or a red Three as the result of the initial turn-up).

In these cases you may only take the pack if you can immediately use the upcard to start a new meld in conjunction with at least two matching *natural* cards from your own hand. (If you have none on the table already, this may count as your initial meld provided it meets the initial meld scoring requirement described below under 'melds'.) Furthermore,

3. The pack is 'stopped' to you personally if the upcard is a black Three. In this case you may not take it at all but can only draw from stock.

Melds: All melds made by one partnership are kept together in one place. Subject to rules governing composition and value of melds, you may in your turn (*a*) start one or more new melds, and/or (*b*) add ('lay off') one or more natural or wild cards to any of your partnership's existing melds. Cards once melded cannot be retrieved for further play.

A meld must contain three or more cards, of which at least two must be natural cards, and not more than three may be wild. All natural cards in a meld must be of the same rank.

A canasta is a meld of seven (or more) cards, and may be melded outright or gradually built up by laying off additional cards to smaller melds. Once completed, the cards of a canasta are squared up in a pile, with a red card face up on top if it is a natural canasta (containing no wild cards), and a black card if it is a mixed canasta (containing one or more wild cards).

A canasta is bound to contain at least four natural cards, but there is no limit to the number of wild cards that may belong or be subsequently added to it. As soon as any wild card is laid off to a natural canasta, remember to replace the top red card by a black one.

Red Threes are not melded. Black Threes may only be melded if you go out on the same turn (*see below*).

Initial meld: The first meld or melds made by a partnership must total a certain minimum value (counting each Joker 50, Ace or Two 20, high card 10, low card 5). What that minimum value is depends on your partnership's cumulative score in the current game, as follows:

Score so far	Required initial value
A minus figure	any
Less than 1500	50
1500 but under 3000	90
3000 or more	120

You may count the combined values of more than one meld towards this minimum requirement, but you may *not* count the 500 or 300 point canasta bonus towards it, nor any bonus deriving from red threes.

(Remember that the pack is frozen to your side until it has made an initial meld of the minimum required value. But the initial meld does not *have* to be made from the hand: provided it meets the requirement it may be made by melding the upcard with at least two natural cards from your hand.)

Discard: Having drawn and either melded or not, you complete your turn by taking a card from your hand and placing it face up on the pack, unless in your turn you go out and have nothing left to discard.

You may not discard a red Three. If you discard a black Three, you thereby freeze the pack to your left-hand opponent for one turn only.

If you discard a wild card you thereby freeze the pack to everybody, and it remains frozen until taken. To show that the pack is frozen, you place the wild card not on the top but at the bottom of the pack, face up and sticking out sideways so that it is clearly visible. (It is, however, still the upcard for one turn and theoretically obscures the card visible on top. This means that your left-hand opponent may *not* immediately capture the pack by matching the visible card with a natural pair from his hand; but as soon as he has played, his discard becomes the upcard and thereafter the pack can be taken in accordance with the rule for capturing a frozen pack.)

End of game by going out. A player goes out and thereby ends the game when in one turn he gets rid of all the cards in his hand – either by melding them all, or by melding them all except one and discarding that last one.

You may not go out unless your side has made at least one canasta. But you can meet this requirement by melding or completing a canasta on the turn in which you go out. It is only when you are going out that you may meld black Threes – either three or four of them.

If after drawing from stock you are in a position to go out, you are permitted (not required) to ask your partner whether it suits him. If you do ask, you must do so before melding any card at all. The correct wording is 'May I go out, partner?', to which he must reply either Yes or No. You are then bound by his reply. (Indeed, if he says Yes and you find that you cannot go out after all, you are penalised 100 points.)

You get a bonus of 100 for 'going out blind', that is, if you personally have not previously melded anything during the course of the current deal. But you only qualify for the bonus if all your cards are meldable in their own right – you don't get it if you lay off cards to your partner's melds.

End of game by exhausting stock. Somebody usually goes out before the stock is used up, but in case they don't, this is what happens: if the last card drawn from stock is a red Three, the player faces it, makes any melds he wishes, but does not discard. That ends the deal.

If not, he plays in the usual way and then discards. The next in turn must then take the pack (by melding the upcard) if he can legally do so; if not, the deal ends. If he can do so, he makes his play and then discards. From now on the 'pack' will only ever consist of the previous player's discard. If on your turn the previous discard matches one of your melds, you are forced to take it, lay it off, and then discard. If it does not match, but can still be melded with the aid of cards from your hand, you may either take no action, in which case the deal ends, or you may make your meld(s), in which case you must discard unless you go out.

This continues until any player in his turn either goes out or fails to take the previous player's discard because legally unable or unwilling to do so.

Scores. Each side reckons its score first for bonuses and then for cards; but note that if a side has melded nothing at all then any red Threes it has count against it instead of for it, their value being combined with the penalty for unmelded cards in hand.

Bonuses

For going out	100
or, for going out blind	200
For each red Three	100
or, for having all four	800
For each natural canasta	500
For each mixed canasta	300

To the score for bonuses is added the total meld value of all melded cards, counting thus:

Cards

Joker	50
Ace, Two	20
High card (K Q J T 9 8)	10
Low card (7 6 5 4 and black 3)	5

From the combined total for bonuses and cards, each side now subtracts the total meld value of all cards remaining unmelded in the hand. (The side that went out, of course, will have cards left only in one hand; the other side will have two handfuls to count against them.)

If a player proves to have a red Three in hand, having failed to expose it on the table, it counts 500 against his side.

Hints on play

Canasta is not one of those Rummy games in which the main object is to 'go out' for the sake of the bonus, regarding melds only as a means to that end. It is one of the other sort, in which the main object is to build up a large score by making as many melds as possible. The side that melds first gains an immediate advantage, having, as it were, hatched the goose that lays the golden eggs, and they should go on exploiting this advantage for all it is worth. As soon as the other side has caught up, the first side should be in or approaching the position at which it has the minimum canasta requirement for going out – not for the sake of using it quickly, but for its power as a threat to the opponents.

When going out has become a real possibility, it may eventually be effected for either of two good reasons: first, that despite your lead and initiative your opponents are now beginning to catch up or even threatening to overtake; or second, that your opponents are so far ahead that going out is your only way of defending against a huge loss. There is a third possible reason – that you have been dealt the sort of hand on which the surprise value of a 'quick out' will produce a small, quick profit for the minimum of intellectual investment – but this does not happen very often, and you need not go out of your way to look for it.

The strategy, then, is to be first to break into the scoring vein, get as much out of it as you can while the going is good, and pull out when your advance begins to lessen – or, if you find yourself on the wrong side, to prevent your opponents from succeeding in the same endeavour, even to the extent of pulling out prematurely if you consider the task hopeless. What about the tactics – the means by which this objective is to be achieved?

Inevitably, this aspect of the game revolves around the taking of the pack (i.e. the discard pile). Even if it contains no more than three or four cards the pack is always advantageous to the player who takes it, and most of your play will be directed towards this end. Usually the first side to take the pack is then able to seize the initiative and dictate the course of the game. If your opponents get it first, you must be prepared to play defensively until you can afford to meet them on their own ground.

Initial meld. At the start of the game your immediate objective is to make the initial meld that will entitle you to set out on your scoring spree. So strive for it – but not at the expense of all other considerations. In particular, try to meld as economically as possible. The fewer cards you keep in hand, the less chance you have of taking the pack, so to use up too many on the initial meld is largely self-defeating. For this reason it is unwise to make your initial meld entirely from the hand: wait until you can meld by taking the pack, and deplete your hand no more than necessary.

In subsequent rounds of play, when your initial meld requirement advances to 90 or 120, you may have to accept the sacrifice of more cards in order to compensate for the extra difficulty of meeting the minimum value. Even so, it is wise to expend no more than four cards for the 90, or six for the 120.

Further melding. Having started, make as many melds as you can, in order to keep up the pressure and increase your ability to take the pack. The more melds you can lay off to, the greater difficulty your opponents have in finding safe discards. Don't be frightened of sullying natural canastas by the addition of wild cards, and do not cripple yourself for the sake of working towards the bonus for going out concealed. If your hand happens to lend itself to that fortunate prospect, all well and good; if not, forget it.

There are circumstances in which restraint is worth exercising on the making of melds. The question of economy is one of them, as it was in the case of the initial meld: don't part with too many cards, and in particular don't part with any which may be of use in capturing the pack later. For the same reason it is also sensible to refrain from melding when the discard pile is large: the more cards you keep in hand the more chance you have of capturing it. Defer melding until the pack has been taken, even if not by yourself.

The importance of completing your first canasta is obvious, as it puts you in a position of constant threat (to go out). It is also important throughout the game not to fall behind in the completion of canastas, for which purpose mixed canastas, though less profitable than natural ones, are infinitely better than none at all.

Freezing the pack. It is a beginner's irritating habit to freeze the pack for no better reason than that he happens to be able to, and can think of nothing else to do. There are, of course, times when it is right to freeze the pack and times when it is wrong.

The most important time to freeze the pack is when your opponents have started melding and you have not, as it is your only effective defence against their ability to keep on recapturing it for continual rewards. Freezing is also a good defensive move when your opponents have too many cards in hand and melds on the table, as it enables you with relative safety to discard their players (cards which match their melds and would otherwise enable them to take the pack) and improve the overall meldability of your own hand.

When the pack is frozen it is good to have a hand containing many pairs, as they give you more opportunity to capture it. This does not mean, however, that a hand full of pairs is a good excuse for freezing the pack. It is obviously undesirable to freeze if there is a high probability that the other side will be able to take it. Finally, avoid freezing just because you are unable to find a safe discard. In such circumstances you are likely to do yourself more harm than good.

Black Threes and other cards. If you can find a better discard than a black Three, make it, and save the Three for the time when it is the only solution to an otherwise impossible position. Given a black Three early in the game, a good time to discard it is often when you have just made an initial meld. Since it freezes the pack to your left-hand opponent only, it prevents him from taking the pack before your partner has a chance to take advantage of the position.

Wild cards should be put to work, not hoarded. Every one added to a meld is a bird in the hand when it comes to the score. And do not lightly discard Aces. They, too, are better put to work.

Discarding. Discard low in early rounds, as such cards are not suitable for initial melds. Watch the discards made by your left-hand opponent and try to match them for as long as you feel he is genuinely throwing away unwanted cards. Since your right opponent will be watching you with the same objective in view, don't make things easy for him by sticking rigidly to the discard of singletons. At judicious times have no hesitation in discarding from three or more, so that when he subsequently discards the same rank you can capture the pack and meld. The only time to concern yourself seriously with your partner's discards is when there is a real danger of your opponents' going out. By matching your partner's discards in this situation you may save yourself a lot of penalties.

The time to discard players of your opponents' melds is when the pack is frozen and they appear to have little chance of capturing it. Any cards that are of no use to you but possibly of use to them are best reserved for discarding until the pack is small.

Going out. We have already noted that going out is more of a defensive measure than anything else, either because you are too far behind and want to cut your losses, or because your opponents are beginning to catch up and you do not want to cut your profit margin. Watch the timing. A good time to go out is when your opponents have too many cards in hand.

Sample game

All Rummy games are difficult to notate and inconvenient to play through in sample form, but Canasta, with 108 cards, is virtually impossible. Here instead is an illustration of the end position of a game, showing how the score is calculated.

FIGURE 7

How your side of the table might look at the end of a game in which you have been looking after the melds made by your own partnership. You have just gone out and score as follows:

300 for the mixed canasta (black Seven on top)
100 for the single red Three
100 for going out
300 total value of cards in your melds
—45 for face value of cards left

in your partner's hand (J-J-T-9-5)
Total: 755. Your opponents have:
200 for two red Threes
100 for cards melded
—150 for cards left in both hands
Total: 150. You win.

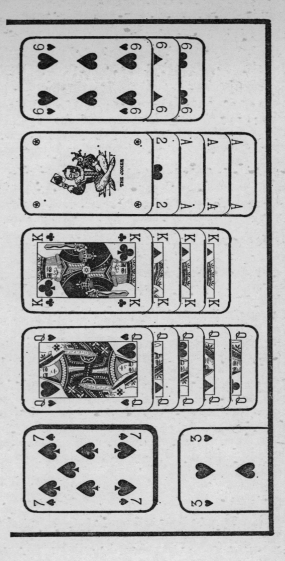

7

CALYPSO
A game of West Indian folk songs

This unusual and undeservedly neglected game was invented in the early fifties by R. B. Willis, who named it after the songs of Trinidad where he was living. In Britain, Calypso was avidly espoused, modified, refined and promoted by Bridge master Kenneth Konstam.

It is easy to see why the game attracted initial enthusiasm. It is designed for four, socially the most acceptable number at a card table; it represents a cross between the objectives of Rummy and the mechanics of Whist, two of the most successful card games ever devised; and, at the same time, it is quite original in its ingenious use of these otherwise well-tried features of card play. Above all, it is extremely simple to learn. For my taste, nothing spoils a potentially good card game so much as showy complications that appear to be introduced for effect, often in default of any real depth.

Why it failed to maintain the following it deserved is less easy to determine. A perhaps over-simplified view is that it arrived at the wrong time. Card players of the fifties had gone to great pains to learn the complications of then-fashionable Canasta, and must have been loath to waste this effort by taking on anything else. Perhaps recent memories of years of austerity worked in favour of a game that covered the table with lots of sumptuous card combinations worth millions of points, rather than one of such spartan simplicity as Calypso.

Whatever the reason, it remains high on my list of games worth reviving. Give it a fair trial and see what you think.

The game

Cards. Four standard 52-card packs, making 208 cards in all; it is desirable, but not essential, that they all be of the same back design and colour. They should, however, all be of the same size.

Game. A game consists of four deals, one by each player in turn, and lasts about half an hour. Scores are not noted until the end of the last deal.

Shuffle and deal. It is convenient for each player to shuffle about a quarter of the composite pack and pass it back to dealer, who shuffles them last as best he may and then places them all in a face-down pile to form a stock. Dealer then takes the top quarter of the stock and deals out 13 cards each, in ones. The rest of the stock remains out of play and unused until the hands of the first deal have been fully played out.

Rank of cards, object of play. Cards rank in traditional order, from high to low A K Q J T 9 8 7 6 5 4 3 2. Each player 'owns' a particular suit, as follows:

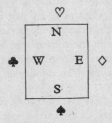

Thus North and South are partners and respectively play hearts and spades against East and West who are respectively associated with diamonds and clubs. Each player's first objective is to collect a complete set of cards, from Ace down to Two, of his own suit. Such a set is called a 'calypso'. Having collected one calypso he can then start collecting another, and so on up to a theoretical maximum of four (because there are four packs in play). His secondary objective is to capture cards that belong to his partner's calypso, as he is permitted to pass cards of his partner's suit across to him when he wins them in a trick. As a third objective, of course, each player will endeavour to prevent players of the opposing partnership from acquiring the cards they need for calypsos in their own suits.

Cards needed for calypsos are captured by winning them in tricks, as described below.

Personal trumps. Before tricks can be played it is essential to understand the way in which 'personal trumps' – a feature unique to Calypso – are used.

The suit that each player is trying to collect is also his personal trump suit. Therefore, when someone leads to a trick he will be leading either from his trump suit (in which case he should announce 'my trump' or something similar), or from one of the others. What happens next depends on which lead is made.

To a non-trump lead each succeeding player must follow suit if possible. The trick is won by the player of the highest card of the suit led. If two identical cards fall to a trick, the first so played ranks higher than the second.

If you cannot follow suit to the card led, you may win the trick by playing any card of your personal trump suit (in which case you should announce 'trump'), or you may lose it by discarding from any other suit. In this case the player of a personal trump wins the trick. If more than one plays from his own personal trump suit, the trick is won by the personal trump of the highest rank (suit does not count for this purpose), and if more than one of the same rank are played then it is the first that takes it.

Note that you can only trump by playing your *own* trump suit, never anyone else's.

To a trump lead each succeeding player must follow suit if possible, and if all do so then the trick is always won by the player who led to it, regardless of rank. In other words, if you lead from your personal trump suit and everyone follows, you automatically win the trick.

If you cannot follow suit to a personal trump lead, then you may win the trick by playing from your own trump suit a card of higher rank than the one led, which can only be overtaken by another player playing a yet higher-ranking card from his own trumps. (You may, of course, lose the trick by playing from a side-suit, but only if you cannot follow.)

In short, when trumps are led the trick is won by the leader unless anyone else legitimately plays a personal trump, in which case the highest-ranking personal trump (or the earliest played of identical ranks) wins the trick.

Tricks and calypsos. The player on the dealer's left leads to the first trick; thereafter the winner of each trick leads to the next. The trick is won by the highest card of the suit led or by the highest personal trump if any are played, except that a trump lead wins the trick regardless of rank unless legitimately over-trumped. Of identical ranks, the first played counts highest.

When you win a trick you first remove from it and place face upwards in front of you any cards of your own suit that you need for building up a calypso – that is, cards of any rank(s) which you have not already got. You may also remove and pass to your partner any card or cards he needs towards his own calypso. However, as only one calypso may be built up at a time, a card that duplicates one already showing in either calypso may not be kept and is lost for the rest of the game. Such duplicates, to-gether with cards of the opponents' suits, are laid aside face downwards to a discard pile. It is convenient for one of the two partners to look after a single common discard pile for his side, rather than to have one each. There is, of course, no need to keep won tricks separate from one another.

There is one exception to the rejection of duplicates. If you win a trick containing several cards of your own (or partner's) suit, as the result of which you can immediately complete your own (or partner's) calypso, you may then complete the calypso and use any surplus cards of the suit to start a new one.

A completed calypso is stacked face up with the Ace on top. The cards of a calypso in the process of being built should be spread face up and in numerical order in a straight line in front of its collector, so that everyone can see which cards it contains and lacks.

End of deal. When 13 tricks have been played, the next 52 cards from stock are taken and distributed singly by the next dealer, that is, the player on the left of the previous dealer. The same procedure is followed in subsequent deals.

Score. The scoring is simple. Each player counts 500 for his first calypso, 750 for his second, and 1000 for any other. He then counts 20 for each card in the calypso he was in course of build-

ing when the game ended. Each partnership's score is found by
adding the two partners' calypso scores together, and finally
adding to that 10 points for every card in their pile of cards won
in tricks.

Hints on play

The play at Calypso is shaped largely by the fact that, although
you must take as many tricks as you can get, you need them not
for their own sake but for the sake of the cards they contain.
Since all cards are good, either because you want them for your
side's calypsos or because you want to keep them from your
opponents, it is correct to play an attacking game, for which
purpose the question of leads when you have the initiative is all-
important. At the same time you must pay particular attention
to how you discard when you do not have the lead and are
unlikely to take the trick yourself. There are good cards to give
to your partner, and bad ones to throw to the opponents.

Your choice is widest when you have the lead, especially at the
start of a new deal. The question is, which suit to play from and
whether to play high or low. As to suits, there are three possibilities: your own, your partner's or either of your opponents'.

Trump lead (own suit). A trump lead, which normally wins the
trick regardless of rank, is standard opening procedure – but it
must be played with understanding. Beginners are tempted to
lead and press their trump suit for as many rounds as it will go
without being overtrumped. This play is faulty. It may well
bring in an average of thirteen cards to your calypso, but so
many are likely to be duplicates, and hence destined for the
waste pile, that it will have been a waste of high trumps to bring
them in.

Given a reasonable holding of trumps, by all means start by
leading them, especially low ones (say Twos to Sixes) that would
be of little value later in the game for purposes of overtrumping.
Leading them is the only chance of putting them to useful work.
High trumps should not be led without due regard to the fact
that they may be more useful for overtrumping at a later stage, or

for winning tricks when your suit is led from other quarters.

Trump leads are inadvisable if you hold the suit too long or too short. With, say, more than six trumps in hand there is a strong possibility that an opponent will be void and take the trick by overtrumping, though of course an Ace lead cannot be overtaken. Three or fewer high-ranking trumps do not invite a trump lead: keep them for overtaking when the suit is led, or for overtrumping when the opportunity arises.

Partner's suit. Not a good lead. Leading partner's suit deprives him of later opportunities to make tricks by trump leads, and unless you can lead an Ace or other master card the chances are nearly two to one against his being able to take it.

An exception to this rule is afforded by the holding of a singleton. If your hand as dealt contains only one card of your partner's suit, and you have a sufficiently early lead, it is good play to lead it in order to create a void that you can trump into (or discard to) later. This play is so obvious as to claim the status of a convention or signal. If it is understood that the lead of a partner's trump implies a void in that suit, the partner stands to gain more by this information than the opponents will.

It should, however, be avoided if you are also weak in your own suit, as you are then less able to take advantage of it yourself by overtrumping.

Adverse suit. The advantage of leading an adverse suit is that only one opponent is in a position to trump it, while the other, whose suit it is, is deprived of later opportunities to make tricks by trump leads.

It is clearly best to lead high; in fact, the lead of a high card in an adverse suit may be regarded as an alternative standard opening to that of a low personal trump. Leading a low adverse trump is justly described by Kenneth Konstam (who refined the mechanics of the game) as 'defeatist', as it is sure to give them the trick and the initiative. One could, however, make a virtue of necessity by proposing a convention that a low adverse lead implies overall weakness.

Which of the two adverse suits makes the better lead? This depends much upon the actual holding, but with comparable strength in both there would be some advantage in leading that of the player on your right, as he will then not be able to trump or overtrump when your partner has played. It is better that the opponent with the greater scope should play before rather than after your partner, so that he can gauge his play accordingly.

If they are not of comparable strength, lead from the stronger, or else from a singleton in order to give yourself a trumpable void.

Other aspects of play. What to play to a trick which you are not winning, or in your estimation are unlikely to win, depends on whether it is going (so far as you can tell) to your partner or to either opponent.

Given a choice of discards, your priorities for throwing to a trick won by partner will be:

1. A card needed for either of your calypsos;
2. A card lacking from an adverse calypso;
3. A low card or singleton from an adverse suit;
4. A duplicate card matching one in either of your side's current calypsos.

Circumstances alter cases, of course. It is obviously better to throw, if you can, the thirteenth card to an adverse calypso than the second to one of your own, especially towards the end of the game. The last card of a calypso is worth at least 260 points, whereas any other is worth only 20 when it comes to the crunch.

If an opponent is winning the trick, you will naturally discard in order of preference:

1. An adverse calypso duplicate;
2. A duplicate in one of your own suits.

Principles of trick play appropriate to such games as Whist and Bridge, in which tricks are collected for their own sake, should not be automatically followed in Calypso. Normally, for example, you discard low when unable to contest a trick in the suit led. In Calypso, it is more appropriate to discard duplicates than to preserve higher ranks. If you can do both, by discarding low-ranking duplicates, so much the better.

Bridge players should resist the automatic temptation to finesse, for the whole process is made practically uncontrollable by the facts that (*a*) there are four cards of each rank, and (*b*) which of them are in play during the course of any given deal – except theoretically the last – is beyond reasonable deduction in the time available. To put it briefly, unless you are last to play never try to take with the King if you can take with the Ace instead. There are occasions on which it may be tried in the suit of the player on your right, but it is nearly always dangerous to try it on in other suits.

Memory plays an important part in the game, but, even if it were possible, you have no need to remember the play of all 208 cards. Normally it is sufficient to regard each deal as complete in itself, bearing in mind that the 52 cards dealt will contain gaps and duplicates. But watch those duplicates, especially if two or three of them attract your eye. If any player is prevented from acquiring all four cards of a given rank he will be unable to complete a single calypso. If it happens to you, all your subsequent play must be directed towards helping your partner make his. Similarly, if you can prevent an opponent from making all four, or even from getting further than his first, it is worth playing towards that tactical objective at the expense of normal rules of procedure.

Sample deal

Let's see how things turn out in the first deal of a sample game, to which West dealt. Cards of each player's trump suit are in bold type.

	N ♡	E ◇	S ♠	W ♣
♡	**9887**	A76	KJ4	T76
◇	AJT43	**QQ93**	865	K973
♠	J3	A9	**AQ43**	Q98
♣	76	KJ82	993	**K65**

North, to lead, starts in his strong adverse suit; at this point it is worth noting that suits will not necessarily be evenly distributed – in this deal, for example, there are sixteen diamonds out but only eleven clubs.

N	E	S	W	
◇ A	◇ Q	◇ 5	◇ 3	East throws a duplicate rank . . .
◇ J	◇ **Q**	◇ 6	◇ 7	. . . and makes the trick with his other Queen, giving him four to his calypso.
◇ 3	◇ **3**	◇ 8	◇ 9	Running the risk of being over-trumped, East makes a low trump lead in order to derive some benefit from his Three. North naturally gives him a duplicate, so East loses one of the four to his calypso.
♠ J	♠ A	♠ 3	♠ 8	East, with good adverse cards, switches to South's suit. North avoids throwing ♠3, as one has already been lost.
♠ 3	♠ 9	♠ A	♠ 9	East might reasonably have switched to hearts; apparently he prefers to void spades, considering this to be his best way of subsequently benefiting from his personal trump Nine.
♣ 7	◇ 9!	♠ 4	♠ Q	South expects to make at least one trump lead, and North, void in the suit but banking on his partner's win, throws a card wanted for an adverse calypso. East's previous move pays off, and he saves the club for his partner.
♡ 8	♡ A	♡ 4	♡ 6	Now East decides to have a go at the other opponent, leading into North's trump.
♡ 7	♡ 6	♡ K	♡ 7	South saves the situation and passes three hearts across to his partner's first calypso. It is hard to see why North gave himself a duplicate – perhaps he meant to play an Eight and his hand slipped.

♣ 6	♣ 8	♣ 9	♣ K	South won't lead trumps for fear that his Queen may be over-trumped, especially by West when there have been no clubs visible yet. East avoids playing ♣ 2 in case he later finds a situation in which it would be better to let West take a trick in clubs.
♡ 9!	♣ K	♣ 3	♣ 5	West is now into his suit (clubs), but to his chagrin North is void and overtrumps. East throws a duplicate, which won't be missed as West already has the King to his first calypso. South, on the other hand, throws a club that would have been useful to it.
♡ 8	♡ 7	♡ J	♡ T	North wins on a personal trump lead, though it stood a strong chance of being overtrumped. But success in this trick is paid for on the next round:
◇ T	♣ 2	♣ 9	◇ K	South could have trumped, but his ♣ 9 would not have been a promising lead for the last trick and since North appears to be winning this one the Queen should give them two instead of only one trick. West, with luck, seizes a club for himself (Two; the Nine is a duplicate) and two diamonds for his partner.
◇ 6	♣ J	♠ Q	♣ 6	West thinks himself fortunate to finish the deal with a trump lead, but South is even more fortunate in being able to overtrump it, adding a Queen to his own calypso and preventing a Jack to West's.

At the end of the first deal, the following part calypsos have been collected:

North   ♡ K J T 9 8 7 6
East   ◇ K Q J 9 8 7 6 3 2
South   ♠ A Q 9 3
West   ♣ K 9 8 7 6 2

And the score so far is North-South 350 (220 in calypsos), East-West 430 (300 in calypsos). In subsequent rounds the initial bias towards diamonds will be counterbalanced in black suits.

8

A game of combinations

Nearly all partnership card games are of the trick-and-trump variety, which is not much variety at all. Canasta is the one exception, although Calypso at least offers a different objective even while it follows the usual tricky mechanics.

For a change of scenery, then, I include a non-trick partnership game of my own devising, which, far from being trumped up for the occasion, has the merit of having been played for about ten years by a group of players who continue to find it varied and challenging.

Concerto is based on the simple idea of calling upon you and your partner to combine your cards into scoring Poker combinations, but without knowing in advance which cards the other holds. The game has nothing to do with Poker as such, nor is it even a gambling game. Poker hands only come into it because they are widely known and happen to suit the mechanics of the game quite well.

It will, I think, appeal particularly to players of partnership games which encourage the play of cards as a means of conveying useful information about the hand from which they come, so that maximum advantage can be derived from that knowledge while there is still time to pursue it.

Concerto can be played haphazardly, of course, as can Whist or Bridge, but it then loses its point. As with Whist, the actual mechanics of the game are exceedingly simple. All the skill lies in the significant play of cards.

The game

Cards and preliminaries. Use a standard 52-card pack. Partners sit opposite each other. Decide who is to deal first by any agreed means. A game consists of four deals, the turn to deal passing to the left on each occasion, and is won by the side with the greater aggregate of points. (Fig. 8 illustrates a recommended score-sheet.)

Shuffle and deal. The cards must be very thoroughly shuffled before each deal. Deal them one at a time and face down until every player has thirteen.

Object. The members of each partnership have 26 cards between them. Their object is to form these into four scoring Poker hands of five cards each, and to avoid being left with a Poker combination amongst the remaining six cards. Cards are played one at a time to the table, and verbal discussion is prohibited. Each partnership plays in turn – there is no interaction of card play between the two partnerships.

Poker hands. A Poker hand by definition consists of any five cards. If these match one another by rank or suit in certain prescribed ways they constitute a scoring Poker combination. From highest to lowest, the combinations and their scores are as follows:

Combination	Score	Explanation
Straight flush	15	Five cards in suit and sequence (e.g. ♠A 2 3 4 5).
Four of a kind	12	Four of the same rank (e.g. ♠5 ♡5 ♣5 ◇5), the 5th any.
Full house	8	Three of one rank plus a pair (e.g. ♠5 ♡5 ♣5 ◇Q ♠Q).
Straight	7	Five in sequence but not all of the same suit.
Flush	6	Five of the same suit but not in sequence.
Three of a kind	3	Three of the same rank, plus two odd cards.
Two pair	2	Two of one rank, two of another, the 5th any.
One pair	1	Two of the same rank, the other three unmatched.

A five-card hand containing no combination scores nothing. For the purpose of a straight or straight flush, Ace may count high or low (either A 2 3 4 5 or T K Q K A), but not intermediate (e.g. Q K A 2 3 is not valid). Poker players may wonder why the straight scores more than the flush. The reason is that in Concerto it is harder to make.

Order of play. The player on the first dealer's left is designated North and his partner South; dealer is West and his partner East. North-South play first, with North leading, while East-West merely sit back and observe. Having made and scored their first combination, North places it in front of him in the manner of a won trick, only face up instead of down, and then East leads to the first East-West hand. Play continues in this order, South leading third, then West, and so on until each player has two Poker hands lying face up on the table before him. These hands are kept face up and slightly spread so that all played cards remain visible – Concerto is not intended to be a memory test, but calls for the application of skill to whatever deductions may be made from visible cards.

Method of play. The leader to each round (North, in the first instance) plays any card from his hand face up to the table. He may not pass. His partner may then either pass or add a card of his own to the first. Play continues in this way, each in turn either passing or adding a card, until five cards have been played to the table. The partners then score for whatever combination they may have made; the leader to the hand lays it face up before him; and the player on his left then leads to the next hand to be made by the opposing partnership.

Passing restrictions. The leader to a hand must play the first card – he is not allowed to pass the lead. Thereafter, each in turn may either play a card or pass, but with the following restriction: if one partner passes, and the other passes back, the first may not pass further but must now play. Thus, although there is no restriction on the number of passes a single player can make in the course of a hand (he may pass on all five turns in order to let his partner play out a ready-made combination), no more than two passes may be made consecutively *between* the two partners. In order not to lose count, it is helpful to say 'pass' or 'pass back' as the case may be; then a 'pass-back' cannot be followed by a 'pass'.

Dropping out. Instead of saying 'pass' or 'pass back', a player may drop out of the hand altogether by saying 'play', in which case his partner must then complete the hand entirely by himself.

Game bonus. When each player has two Poker hands lying before him the play ceases and each side totals its four scores. Whichever side has the greater total adds 10 points for game. In the event of a tie, the 10-point game bonus is temporarily held back until the residual bonus has been scored.

Residual bonus. Each side will have six unplayed cards left over, which must now be exposed on the table. Each partnership then examines the other's cards, rejects any one of them from consideration, and scores five times the value of any combination formed by the remaining five cards. (For example, if one side is left with ♠3, ♡Q 3, ♣Q J 2, the other will discount the Jack or the Two and score a residual bonus of 10, being five times the value of a two-pair combination.) If three pairs are left, a sixth card is *not* rejected and the opponents score a residual bonus of 15.

Total score. If the game bonus was held in abeyance because of a tie in the play, it now goes to the side which scored the greater residual bonus. If this also resulted in a tie, it goes to the side that played the first card of the deal. Each side totals its hand score and bonuses (if any), and the result is carried forward towards game.

Hints on play

Whether or not your side has good combinations available depends upon the luck of the deal, but whether or not you succeed in extracting your best possible combinations depends entirely on how well you play your cards. In the long run – and a rubber of four games is long enough for the purpose – the side which made

	N-S	E-W	
1	12	8	1
2	7	15	2
3	12	7	3
4	8	12	4
total	39	42	
game	-	10	
bonus	-	5	
TOTAL	39	57	

FIGURE 8

Concerto score-sheet, showing the actual scores for the illustrative game which follows.

the better play will win, and the luck of the deal will hardly enter into it. What this amounts to is that a partnership needs to play to a system, whereby the cards each one plays and the order in which he plays them conveys information about the rest of his hand. The need for such a system will be evident from a simple example. Suppose you are to lead, and you hold:

♠ J T 9 7 ♡ A K 9 ♣ 9 6 3 ♢ Q 5 2

You cannot afford to miss a straight flush if one is possible, and your best chance lies in the spade holding, for which you require your partner to hold either ♠ 8 or, more remotely, ♠ K ♠ Q. If he cannot help, then your next best possibility is of making four Nines, for which you require him to hold ♢ 9. Is it possible to play in such a way as to communicate all three possibilities to him, so that he will know whether to play or pass, and if so what to play, while retaining the opportunity to make either a straight flush or four of a kind from the same lead? As we shall see later, the answer is 'yes', provided that you employ a good signalling system by which to do it. First, however, there are some general points to consider.

Distribution of cards. On average, you and your partner can expect to have a straight flush available between you about twice in every five deals, and four of a kind twice in every three. You are bound to hold several middling combinations between you every time (full houses, straights and flushes). It is remotely possible not to have a straight – key cards for which are Fives and Tens; a side with none of either can make no straight – but you will almost invariably have at least three flushes. You would be unusually lucky to hold a ready-made straight flush or four of a kind in your own hand, but the holding of several middling combinations is so usual as to be unremarkable.

The strategy of the game, then, is based on aiming for high combinations first (straight flushes, fours of a kind), and 'converting' these to middling combinations (respectively straights or flushes, and full houses) should the high ones prove unattainable. Low combinations, of pairs or threes, are usually made by accident, and only on the fourth hand. To make no combination at all is a disgrace!

In any given deal, the fall of the cards may tend to favour either long combinations (straights and flushes) or short combinations (things of a kind), and this bias will be shown in the cards of both partnerships. If your opponents start by making a straight flush, the chances are that you may be able to make one too; if they start with four of a kind, there is a fair probability that fours and full houses will figure more prominently than straight and/or flush combinations. Your own hand of cards will give you some indication of which way the bias lies, and you should play accordingly.

Playing and passing. Always lead from the strongest part-combination you have in your hand. Four consecutive cards to a straight flush, for example, is stronger than three of a kind, as there are (except at extremes) two possible cards by which your partner can fill it as opposed to only one for the potential quartet.

The same applies throughout the play of a single hand. At any given stage of the play there is always a best combination that can be made from the card or cards so far played. If you can contribute a card which belongs to that best possibility, play it. If not, pass, in case your partner can further it himself. If he cannot do so either, then he will either start to 'convert' by playing a card to the second best combination that can be made from it, or else pass back to you, in which case, knowing he cannot help, you may convert it yourself.

Do not drop out (by saying 'play') unless you are absolutely certain that your partner has a ready-made combination or can successfully complete the one in progress, for, if he cannot, you may thereby force him to play a card he might otherwise have preferred to retain. This call should only be used when your partner has signalled the fact that he has the best possible cards for the current hand.

There is one occasion on which it is virtually obligatory to pass, and that is when your partner, as leader, has played his first card. A single card tells you nothing. You must pass in order to give him a chance to indicate to you what sort of hand he is aiming for. If, for example, he leads ♡6 and you hold ♡5 ♡4, do not play them until you are sure he is aiming for a straight flush. He would not thank you for a failed straight flush if he were playing from four Sixes! It is not until the leader has played his second card that his partner knows what combination he is playing from. Two cards in suit and range (i.e. potentially belonging to the same straight) signal his intention of a straight flush; two of the same rank signal his intention of trying for four of a kind. Only play immediately if you yourself can turn that first card into a top combination without further assistance, and even then you should wait for his second card before converting a straight flush into four of a kind (which you can afford to do, since the four-combination includes one unmatched card).

Generally, it is the leader to a hand who takes responsibility for directing it and taking the initiative in making conversions throughout the play. The follower to a hand may pass out of caution; the leader may play out of boldness. The roles should only be reversed if the leader passes back on his second turn, having played only one card – this is a signal indicating that he has a weak hand and is leaving it to you to make the decisions.

Finally, note that although there is no direct interaction between the opposing partnerships, you may derive much benefit from observing not only what cards your opponents play but also which ones they fail to play. Suppose, for example, they start with a potential straight flush by playing ♠9 8 7 5, and then convert it into a flush. Holding three Sixes yourself, there is a good chance that your partner has the fourth, otherwise the opponents would have played it for a straight and scored an extra point. If on your next turn you lead a Six, your partner, who is as wide awake as you are, would be justified in dropping his Six instead of making the conventional opening pass.

Because one side can make deductions from observing cards played by the other, the possibility does exist of bluffing your opponents by playing 'wrong' cards, provided you can do so without otherwise spoiling the hand. This, however, is a highly advanced tactic.

Signals. For consistent success at Concerto you and your partner must either be completely telepathic or follow some sort of signalling system whereby the structure of your hand may be communicated by the cards you play and the order in which you play them. Those of us who play the game regularly have devised a series of signals that work sufficiently well in practice to be considered as more or less standard. Here it must suffice to concentrate only on the major signals and to express them, for conciseness, as if they were invariable rules – which they are not. With experience of the game you will soon learn when and how to break them, and quite possibly you will devise other and even better signals of your own.

You make a signal when you have the lead. Since it is virtually obligatory for your partner to pass after your first card, a signal is formed by the first two cards you play.

If the best feature of your hand is three or more cards to a straight flush, make a straight flush signal, which consists of two cards of the same suit and in the same range.

If you hold four of a kind, play the 'fours' signal, which is two cards of the same rank, but of particular suits as explained below.

If the likeliest possibility you hold is two (or more) sets of three of a kind, play the 'two threes' signal, which is also two cards of the same rank, but of particular suits as explained below.

There is also a 'nothing-better-than-a-full-house' signal.

Ready-made straights and flushes are not worth signalling, so if you have anything less than the combination possibilities outlined above you play the 'no go' signal, which is one card followed by a pass.

STRAIGHT FLUSH SIGNALS

The left-hand side of the following table shows all the possible patterns in which you might hold three or more cards belonging to the same straight flush. X denotes a card held, 0 denotes a gap in your sequence, and the order is high-low from left to right. Thus, for example, X X 0 0 X denotes some such holding as J T – – 7 , while X 0 X X represents some such holding as J – 9 8. The Xs in bold type are the cards to play.

No. of cards in range	Pattern of holding (high–low)	Signal
5	**X X X X** X	L 3 H
4	**X X X** X	L 2 H
	X **X X** 0 X	H 1 L
	X 0 **X X** X	L 1 H
	X **X** 0 **X** X	H 2 L (*two ways*)
3	**X X** 0 0 X ⎫	
	X X 0 X ⎬	H 0 L
	X X X	H 0 L *or* L 0 H
	X 0 **X X** ⎫	
	X 0 0 **X X** ⎬	L 0 H
	X 0 X 0 **X**	H 3 L

On the right-hand side, H-L means play the higher card first and then the low, L-H means play the lower and then the higher. The figure between shows the number of ranks lying between the two signal cards. Thus 'H2L' means 'high card first, two ranks missing, low card second' (e.g. Jack then Eight), while LOH means 'two consecutive cards (no ranks missing), low then high'.

A general principle to be observed in these signals is that you should avoid playing across a gap if at all possible. Only two patterns require you to do so, namely X X 0 X X (e.g. J T – 8 7) and X 0 X 0 X (e.g. J – 9 – 7). The first of these compensates for it by giving you a choice of two (e.g. J, 8 or T, 7); the second offers no compensation but is the worst possible holding anyway.

Reference to the sample hand quoted earlier will not only illustrate the signal in use but also show why it is best to avoid playing across a gap. Given that hand and the lead, your partner would play first ♠J and then ♠9. The signal is H1L, from which you infer that he holds ♠J T 9 – 7 and wants the Eight. Naturally you will play ♠8 if you have it, and be assured of the straight flush. If not, you could still play successfully if you held ♠K and ♠Q, for by *not playing across the gap* represented by the Eight, your partner has allowed for the remoter possibility of making ♠K Q J T 9. If you cannot help either combination, you pass. Now, if you will refer back to that hand, he knows that a straight flush is not possible and can therefore play another Nine. The cards on the table show ♠J ♠9 ♡9, and it is clear from his signal that if you hold a Nine you can play it and expect to make four of a kind, the ♠J remaining as the idle or unmatched card.

FOUR OF A KIND SIGNAL

Given the lead and a ready-made four of a kind in your hand, play two of them, the first from a red suit, the second from a major suit (♠ and ♡ are major, ♣ and ◇ minor, as at Bridge) – e.g. play ♡ ◇ or ♡ ♣ or ◇ ♣. The full set of signals attaches a different 'meaning' to each of these possibilities, but this is enough to be getting on with.

TWO THREES

Lacking three to a straight flush, or four of a kind, the next best possibility in your hand would be two sets of three of a kind, either of which may, with luck, produce four of a kind with your partner's assistance. The signal for two threes is two cards of the same rank, in any suit combination *other than* the 'red-major' signal for four of a kind. Further refinement of this signal enables you to communicate to your partner the exact rank of the other set of three.

FULL HOUSE

If the best you hold is three of a rank and one or more pairs, you still have a chance of leading into four of a kind. Play two cards of different colour suits, the first from your set of three, the second from a pair. Your partner will play from the first rank if he holds the fourth card, from the second rank if he holds the other two of it.

PLAY AND PASS

If the best you hold is three of a kind and no pairs, play a red card from the set of three and then pass on your second turn. If you hold nothing better than pairs, play a black card (from a pair) and pass. Either of these allows four of a kind to be made if available, and is therefore often a better bet than playing from a ready-made straight or flush. There are also 'straight-or-flush' signals, but these may be left to the imagination.

Practice. One advantage of the lack of direct interaction between the two partnerships is that you can devise and practise signals with a prospective partner. Just deal thirteen cards each, leaving the other twenty-six unseen, and play out your four hands. Test the efficacy of your signals and brilliance of your play by (a) noting what score you actually made for the four hands, (b) calculating what is the best score you could have made had you been able to see all twenty-six cards from the outset, and (c) expressing the former as a percentage of the latter. An average of 75 per cent or more is quite good.

You should always make at least 27 points in the four hands you make between you – anything less is an indicator of less-than-perfect play. It is reasonable to be left with two pairs amongst your six residual cards, but anything more denotes faulty play. That is why the game bonus is set at 10 points – it permits you a penalty of up to two pairs without enabling your opponents to get ahead of your higher score for the better group of four hands.

Doubling. As an optional variant, one partnership may double the game bonus from 10 to 20, and the other re-double it to 40, before play begins. In the event of a tie, the bonus then goes to the opponents of the side that doubled or re-doubled.

Sample game

```
North   ♠984 ♡Q75 ♣98 ◇Q8763
South   ♠A652 ♡A983 ♣QJ76 ◇9

East    ♠KJT ♡JT2 ♣AT3 ◇KJ54
West    ♠Q73 ♡K64 ♣K542 ◇AT2
```

N	S	
◇8	—	South makes the statutory pass.
◇7	—	North calls for two lower diamonds, so pass again;
♠8	♡8	North converts to four of a kind and South can now help.
♣8		
12		N-S score for four of a kind.

E	W	
♠T	—	
♠J	—	East calls for two higher spades, so West must pass;
◇J	—	West still cannot help.
♡J	—	
♡T	—	
8		

E-W make a full house on their first round. Had East played a Ten instead of a Jack they would have made four of a kind. There was no way of knowing this, but, with a more refined system of play, East might have passed on his third turn to indicate that he held three of each rank, in which case West would have played the Ten. In the actual play, a good principle is followed: all other things being equal, it is better for one person to play more cards out than the other throughout the game, since the player with more in hand at the end can exercise control over breaking up residual combinations. The worst end situation is to have three each.

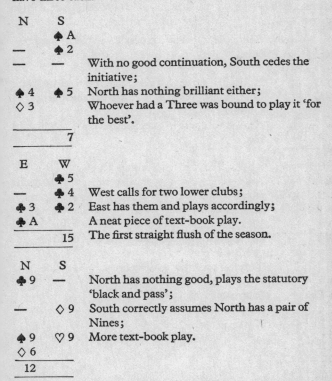

N	S	
	♠ A	
—	♠ 2	
—	—	With no good continuation, South cedes the initiative;
♠ 4	♠ 5	North has nothing brilliant either;
◇ 3		Whoever had a Three was bound to play it 'for the best'.
	7	

E	W	
	♣ 5	
—	♣ 4	West calls for two lower clubs;
♣ 3	♣ 2	East has them and plays accordingly;
♣ A		A neat piece of text-book play.
	15	The first straight flush of the season.

N	S	
♣ 9	—	North has nothing good, plays the statutory 'black and pass';
—	◇ 9	South correctly assumes North has a pair of Nines;
♠ 9	♡ 9	More text-book play.
◇ 6		
12		

An unexpected four of a kind. Why did North automatically play the fifth (unmatched) card? In accordance with the principle that any odd cards should be played by the player holding fewer in hand, so that the residual six should not be evenly divided between them.

E	W	
◇ 4	—	
◇ 5	◇ 2	Not a signal, because ◇ 6 7 8 are out of play
—	◇ A	
—	♠ 3	
	7	

N	S	
	♣ 6	South plays 'black and pass' from his strongest suit.
◇ Q	♣ Q	North plays from his best; South can only copy.
♡ Q	—	South must pass in case North has the fourth Queen.
—	♠ 6	North must pass in case South has a Six, which he has.
	8	

E	W	
	♣ K	
♠ K	♡ K	East seizes the initiative for justifiable reasons;
◇ K	—	West passes, having no combination to break up.
♣ T	—	East discards the Ten, knowing that there is another in play.
	12	This last hand was a lucky break.

The result of the game is as follows:

N-S	E-W	
12	8	
7	15	
12	7	
8	12	
39	42	for combinations
	10	for game
	5	to E-W for the pair of Sevens left in their opponents' hands
39	57	– an unusually high-scoring game.

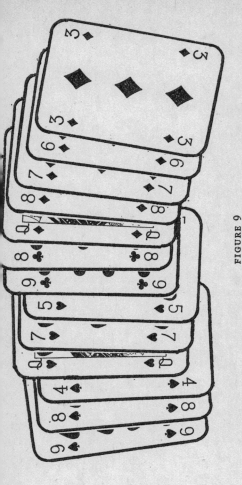

FIGURE 9

Given this hand (North's in the illustrative game above) you are concerned to make either a straight flush in diamonds, built upon your 8-7-6, or, hopefully, four Eights if this fails. You therefore lead ◇8 then ◇7, and, if South passes, continue with another Eight. Now suppose South had the lead, and opened with ♡8. Theoretically, you could immediately play an Eight instead of passing, to show that you can complete the quartet. But this would be over-hasty. For all you know, he may be playing from ♡ J T 9 8, in which case he would next play ♡J and you would add your ♡7 for the straight flush. Wait for his second card before stepping in and making the conversion to four Eights. For more detailed signalling, see the chapter on Concerto in the author's book of *Original Card Games*, Batsford, 1977.

PART II

SOLO AND CUT-THROAT GAMES

The term 'cut-throat' usually denotes any game in which each person plays for himself, as distinct from a game of fixed partnerships. But it is convenient to recognise a third category under the general description 'solo', in which, although each plays for himself in the long run, temporary partnerships are formed from deal to deal as one player (the soloist) undertakes to play his hand against the combined efforts of the others to beat him. Such games may be said to combine the best of both worlds, providing opportunities for the application of both solo and partnership skills.

9 SOLO WHIST
A game of individualists

Solo Whist is a popular English gambling game in which one player takes on or 'declares a contract against' the other three, in contrast to the two-against-two structure of classical partnership Whist.

For all its popularity, the game has not attracted as much serious attention as its high qualities undoubtedly merit. Two possible causes of neglect might be suggested. One is that, as an essentially gambling game, it lacks a scoring system of sufficient refinement to appeal to card-players (such as myself) who will not play for money. Another possible demerit may attach to its name. 'Solo Whist' unconsciously suggests a derivative, even a perversion, of some such imaginary concept as 'proper' Whist. This is not so, and the relation between the two games is far from direct. Partnership Whist, though French in origin, is essentially an English development dating back to the seventeenth century. Solo, on the other hand, bears closer relation to the nineteenth-century popular game of Boston, and is widely played in the Low Countries. It may even be described as the national game of Belgium, and in older sources is referred to as Whist de Gand, or Ghent Whist. This circumstance also helps to explain the French terminology particularly associated with the game.

There are two forms of Solo – the classic form described here, and a later development called Auction Solo, which is outlined in an appendix to this chapter. As might be expected, modern Auction Solo is a souped-up version of the original, said to have been designed for greater variety and excitement. There is no universally accepted standard form of either game. The following may therefore be regarded as 'textbook Solo', from which the actual practice of individual schools may differ in various details.

The game

Cards. A standard 52-card pack. Cards rank in their normal order, from high to low A K Q J T 9 8 7 6 5 4 3 2.

Preliminaries. Establish seats and right of first deal by any agreed means. Each deal is usually regarded as a separate event and is settled in chips, of which each player should start with not fewer than twenty. Alternatively, settlements can be recorded in writing (this serving as a crude sort of scoring system). Each new deal is made by the player on the left of the previous dealer, and all play rotates clockwise around the table.

Shuffle and deal. Anyone may shuffle, but the dealer has the right to shuffle last. Deal cards in batches of three at a time to each player, followed by a single card to make thirteen each. The last card of the pack, which belongs to the dealer, must be turned face up on the table. The suit of the turn-up is the 'preferred' trump suit, and as soon as the suit has been positively accepted or rejected as trump the card is taken up into the dealer's hand.

Object. There is a round of bidding to establish which player will undertake a contract against the other three, although there is also a bid – the lowest – by which one player calls on anyone else to support him in a partnership contract against the other two. The values, names and explanations of the possible bids are tabulated here and detailed opposite.

PROP AND COP
The general idea is that this partnership game is only played if no-one has a hand good enough to venture a positive bid on his own: thus the player who can make four tricks in the preferred trump, but not the five needed for a solo bid, has a chance to 'propose', and if anyone else finds himself in the same position he will 'accept' – hence the fixing of the contract at eight tricks (theoretically four each). Some schools of thought do not recognise 'prop and cop', and abandon the deal if no-one bids solo. This practice may be condemned as pointless.

Value	Bid (colloquial in parentheses)	Object
2	Proposal and acceptance (*prop and cop*)	Partners take 8 tricks with preferred trump
2	Solo	Caller takes 5 tricks with preferred trump
3	Misère	Caller takes 0 tricks at no trump
4	Abondance (*abundance*)	Caller takes 9 tricks with own trump
4	Abondance royale (*royal abundance*)	Caller takes 9 tricks with preferred trump
6	Misère ouverte (*spread misère*)	Caller takes 0 with hand of cards exposed
8	Abondance déclarée (*declared abundance*)	Caller takes 13 tricks at no trump (or with own trump if previously agreed – see note)

SOLO

The caller, playing against the other three, must win at least five tricks, and must accept the preferred suit as trumps.

MISÈRE AND OPEN MISÈRE

Playing without a trump suit, the caller must take no tricks. As soon as he is forced to take a trick he loses his contract without further play. If he considers the hand unbeatable he will play 'open', in which case he spreads his hand of cards face up on the table, though not until the first trick has been played and taken.

ABONDANCE AND ROYAL ABONDANCE

A player bidding 'abondance' must win at least nine of the thirteen tricks. He has the privilege of choosing his trump suit, which may or may not be that of the turned up card, but he does not announce his intended trump suit until the first card is about to be led to the first trick (and, of course, if overcalled by a higher bid he does not announce it at all).

Royal abondance has exactly the same object as abondance, and is merely a bid which enables one player to overcall another who has already bid abondance by offering to take nine tricks using the suit of the turn-up as trumps. If the first bidder was intending to nominate the preferred suit anyway, he can establish priority by announcing that fact, in which case he is not overcalled by the bidder of royal abondance. (Not all authorities agree on this point; many do not even notice that the problem exists.)

DECLARED ABONDANCE

The caller of declared abondance must win all thirteen tricks, and has the privilege (obligatory) of leading to the first trick. Strictly speaking, a declared abondance must automatically be played without a trump suit. In some schools, it is never played at no-trump, but the caller nominates his own trump suit; and in yet other schools this can be overcalled by a bid of declared abondance in the preferred trump. There is no point in such complication, as the bid occurs too rarely to make competition worth while. Players should agree beforehand which system to follow.

Bidding procedure. Starting with the player on the dealer's left, each in turn must either pass or make any bid higher than one that has gone before. Once a player has passed he may not re-enter the bidding, except for the purposes of 'prop and cop' as explained below. As soon as a positive bid has been followed by three passes, that bid is established and the play begins.

If one player proposes, and if the proposal has not been over-called by a solo or higher bid, a subsequent player may bid by saying 'accept'; and if this in turn is not overcalled by a solo or a higher bid, the proposer and acceptant are then obliged to play. (Tricks are still played clockwise around the table – it does not matter if the partners are not opposite each other.)

If eldest hand (the first to bid) passes, and the only other bid made is a proposal, then eldest is permitted to accept if he wishes, in spite of having passed the first time. This privilege of accepting after having passed does *not* apply to any other player.

If a proposal is followed by three passes, there being no acceptant, the proposer may then either raise his bid to a solo or else pass.

If all players pass, 'text-book procedure' is to abandon the hands and let the deal pass to the left. In practice, many schools play one of several varieties of 'all-against-all' games with the hands as dealt, of which the version recommended here is called...

COMPETITIVE MISÈRE

Tricks are played at no trump. The player who takes the most tricks is the loser, and pays the others one unit each.

Play. Before the opening lead is made, the dealer takes up his faced card, and, if the contract being played is abondance, the caller announces the trump suit. The lead to the first trick is always made by eldest hand (the player on the dealer's left) except in a declared abondance, when it is made by the caller. If an open misère is being played, the caller does not expose his cards until the first trick has been played and taken.

The usual rules of trick-taking apply. Follow suit to the card led if possible; if not possible, either trump or discard. The trick is taken by the highest card of the suit led, or by the highest trump if any are played, and the winner of one trick leads to the next.

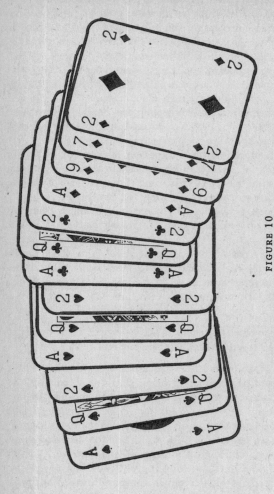

FIGURE 10

The importance of position. This hand is good for a solo if diamonds are turned, as you can reckon on making at least one of the Queens. In any other suit the hand is biddable if you play fourth to the first trick, but risky if you lead.

Settlement. The value of each game is as follows: Solo 2, Misère 3, Abondance or Royal Abondance 4, Open Misère 6, Declared Abondance 8. If the caller wins his game he receives the appropriate value from each player; if he loses, he pays the appropriate value to each player.

There are various methods of settlement for 'prop and cop', of which the simplest is for each member of the winning partnership to receive two units, one from each member of the losing partnership.

A quasi-score may be kept by noting the settlement in writing, preceding each figure by (+) or (−). A figure must be noted against each player's initial on every deal, and the minuses (of course) should always cancel out the plusses.

Example

S	W	N	E	
−4	+12	−4	−4	Successful abondance by West
+2	+2	−6	+2	Failed solo by North
−2	−2	+2	+2	Successful prop and cop by North and East (or failed by South and West).
−3	+1	+1	+1	Competitive misère: South took most tricks.
−7	+13	−7	+1	*Result*

Hints on play

Solo Whist is a subtle game in which it is easy to err in either of two directions – that of excessive caution, and that of extreme recklessness. The over-cautious player will never take a chance on a reasonable but not foolproof bid which the more experienced or imaginative player will undertake promptly; the reckless player will undertake too many long-shot hands and come off worst. If all players are cautious, as usually happens with beginners, the game is dull because there are few bids. This danger is best overcome by playing a Competitive Misère when all pass, as those who lose by taking the most tricks will thereby learn to recognise strength in hand when they see it. If one player is reckless, the game is dull because he hogs the limelight, preventing others from taking a hand with their more reasonable bids, and his frequent losses will be a foregone conclusion. (What makes any game exciting is the fight, not the defeat.) Since dullness can therefore be caused by one reckless player, though not by one cautious player, some argue in favour of playing for money in that the expense incurred discourages reckless overbidding. The point is arguable, in both senses of the word.

Before considering the individual bids that may be made, note first the one important respect in which Solo differs from Bridge, Whist and the majority of other trick-taking games in English card tradition. This lies in the fact that cards are dealt in batches of three, with the result that a balanced distribution of cards amongst the four players is the exception rather than the rule. In Bridge and Whist you normally expect to find the cards of your own hand distributed 4-3-3-3 or 4-4-3-2 amongst the suits, so that any suit longer than five or shorter than two gives you a hand well worth thinking about. In Solo, a hand of the pattern 7-4-2-0 may well give you a good bid, but should not be regarded as anything out of the ordinary. Whether or not the hand is biddable depends not on the distribution but on the quality of the cards you hold.

With this point in mind it is fairly easy to indicate the difference between a slightly risky bid and an out-and-out long shot. A slightly risky bid is one which you will only lose if the remaining cards are unfavourably distributed against you in your opponents' hands. Such a bid is worth making. A long shot is one which you can only win if the remaining cards are distributed amongst the others in your favour. Such a bid is not worth making.

When you are not the caller, remember that you are playing as a member of a partnership of three, and not just for the pleasure of making as many tricks as you can yourself (or losing them, in the case of a misère). It is always to the advantage of the caller's opponents – who, in accordance with card tradition, but in defiance of logic, are known as the defenders – to lead through the caller rather than up to him. In other words, the lead to a trick is always best made by the player on the caller's right, so that he has to play second. Caller's preferred position to a trick is either first (leader) or fourth; the others should therefore play as far as possible to deny him this advantage.

When defending a positive (non-misère) bid, lead low through the caller, and try as much as possible to weaken his hand either by leading trumps or by forcing them out of him by leading suits in which he is void. If playing from a sequence (e.g. from Q J T etc.) always take with the lowest but lead with the highest – though, if you hold Ace, King, lead the King. By following these and other principles derived from partnership Whist your co-defenders will be able to deduce useful features of your hand and play accordingly.

Keeping track of the cards played is important. You need not remember them all, but try at least to count the trumps as they appear, to keep track of the Aces and Kings, and to note when anyone else has a void suit.

Proposal and acceptance

Some schools do not allow the bids of proposal and acceptance, admitting nothing lower than a solo, possibly on the grounds that 'it is too easy to make'. This view is mistaken. If a particular school does find 'prop and cop' too predictably successful, it means they are playing too cautiously and passing up hands on which more experienced players would go solo. The whole point of aiming for eight tricks between two players is that neither of them adjudges his hand good enough for five on its own.

It is to be generally understood – as a matter of convention, but born of common sense – that the player who proposes has some strength in trumps, though not necessarily enough to justify a solo bid. It follows that a player who accepts need not himself have strength in trumps, but should be able to offer further support, especially in side-suits. If neither partner feels strong enough to lead trumps the bid was probably risky, and the defenders will take advantage of this reluctance, when they spot it, to lead trumps themselves.

Position is of some importance in the bidding, and especially so in respect of 'prop and cop'. The best position from which to accept is a fourth hand, as the fact that the proposal has not been overcalled by a solo bid bodes well for the partnership contract. It is risky to accept eldest hand's proposal as second hand, as the third and fourth to bid may well let the contract stand for the sheer pleasure of defeating it.

As eldest hand (first to bid), do not feel obliged to propose if your cards are only just biddable. If your hand is not strong enough for an independent bid, you may safely pass, since you still retain the opportunity to accept should one of the other players propose – a circumstance which automatically suggests that your hand may be stronger than you think. Alternatively, you may well propose on a hand which may or may not be quite good enough for a solo. If a later player accepts, you have a playable game; if not, and all pass, then you may reasonably consider raising your bid to a solo, knowing that it cannot be overcalled.

Here is a hand on which eldest passed, but subsequently accepted a proposal (spades trump):

♠K Q T 4 ♡K 2 ♣T 8 5 4 ◇8 5 2

The proposer's hand was:

♠87653 ♡A ♣A976 ◇T96

This is the sort of combination that makes it criminal to abolish 'prop and cop'!

If you and your partner are sitting side by side, the ideal positioning is for one to be leading to a trick to which the other is playing fourth. As the contracting side, with presumed strength in trumps, you should lead trumps early in order to draw them from your opponents and so establish your side-suits. Against this, however, you should avoid forcing your partner to play trumps if you are weak in them yourself. As in partnership Whist, note what suit your partner leads first, and return it when convenient to do so. Lead from strength – either trumps, or from your strongest suit, whichever you want returned. It is not particularly desirable to lead a singleton.

Solo. Solo is a bid to win five tricks in the preferred trump suit. In order to bid it, you need to have a hand that will enable you to win a certain five tricks in the turned trump. This may sound so obvious as to be trivial, but nevertheless in defiance of all probabilities there are players who will quite happily bid solo, in spades, on a hand such as:

♠K Q 9 4 ♡8 ♣A K Q J 3 ◇T 9 8

The idea is to make two trumps, one of them on a heart lead after the Eight has gone; at least the top two clubs; and one for luck, in either trumps or clubs. Without the lead, a probable outcome is the win of two trumps as anticipated, the possible win of ♣A when led, and, if very lucky, the possible win of ♣K, for a final result of four or even only three tricks. 'Yes,' says one commentator, who shall be nameless; 'Solo is easy enough; just look for five near-certain tricks.'

At the other extreme, there are players so mesmerised by Aces that they will pass up a perfectly feasible solo bid for lack of them – as, for example, on the following hand, again with spades turned:

♠K J 9 8 7 5 2 ♡5 ♣J 9 4 ◇Q 3

Given the lead, this is a good example of the 'slight risk' which we defined previously as being worth taking. With seven trumps in hand, the holder can afford to lose two of them in the not unreasonable hope that those same two tricks will clear the defenders out of their three top trumps (Ace, Queen and Ten). Correct strategy, therefore, is to lead the King.

Even without the lead, you could safely bid solo (spades, again, for convenience) on:

♠K Q T 8 7 6 ♡K T 9 8 ♣K 4 2 ◇—

The side-suit Kings should produce two tricks, the void in diamonds brings in a low trump, and the remaining five trumps are good for the outstanding two.

What, in general, are the minimum requirements for a biddable solo?

The first merit is length or strength in trumps, counting as part of this assessment any void or singleton side-suit which can be ruffed with a low one at the appropriate time. On trumps alone, the borderline between a doubtful and a feasible solo is finely drawn. For instance, a holding of A K Q 9 and one lower is risky, whereas A K Q T and one might be expected to succeed without inducing gasps of astonishment. When holding five trumps, always calculate on the pessimistic assumption that at least one defender may hold five as well. Even a seven-card suit should be headed by nothing less than K J 9.

In side-suits, the chief merit is strength and shortness (not length). The expected failure of the first hand quoted above lies in the undue length of the club suit – A K Q J 3, five in all. The most favourable possible distribution of the outstanding eight is 3-3-2, which means that someone will certainly be trumping by the time you have drawn the odd two with the Ace and King. A more probable distribution is 4-3-1, giving you the Ace but not the King, while there is a strong chance (given the unbalanced distribution of your own hand) of one defender's being void, thus depriving you even of the Ace.

With strength and universal shortness – that is, an unusually even distribution of suits – you may even dispense with strength in trumps. The fact that spades is the turned card does not prevent the following holding from offering a good solo:

♠5 4 3 2   ♡A K 2   ♣A K 2   ◊A 3 2

Of course, it will be beaten if any defender is void in diamonds or holds only one heart or club, but the evenness of the suit distribution in your own hand is good enough to lower the probability of such an event to the acceptable level of 'slight risk'.

Some hands make acceptable solos only if you have the lead; others really require to be led up to. For example, consider the trump holding A K Q T 2 in a hand which does not include a void or easily voidable (singleton) suit. The problem card is the Jack. If you have the lead, you can play out the top trumps in order and without undue optimism hope that the Jack will fall by the time the Queen is out, leaving Ten high and a certain trick with the Two, and giving enough for solo even without side-suit support. Without the lead, the missing Jack is a permanent nuisance. By the time you have voided your short suit you run the danger of ruffing low with the Two and finding it overtaken by a higher trump. On the other hand, a holding that lacks Aces but can place reliance on guarded Kings in short suits will work best if you do not have the lead.

In defending against a solo it is good practice to lead a singleton to the first trick (in which respect the game differs from partnership Whist and also from the play at a 'prop and cop' contract in Solo, where a singleton lead is not to be recommended). With a fairly even distribution, a low trump is also not a bad lead. Otherwise, lead your best card – from not too long a suit – and the highest of a sequence, unless you hold Ace, King, in which case play the King.

Abondance and royal abondance. An abondance is a solo, only more so. As before, you must have length and strength in trumps; in addition, you should have a strong, lengthy side-suit and at least one void. Because the dealing system, 3-3-3-1, produces uneven distributions easily, double voids are not uncommon, and a strong two-suited hand is often a must for abondance.

Since the object of the bid is to make at least nine tricks, one way of assessing the hand is to identify the four cards you can afford to lose – and to make sure there are not five of them (otherwise, you make what is known as an 'eight-trick abondance', which comes expensive).

Given two suits of equal length, do not automatically entrump the stronger. Quite often the 'weaker' suit is not merely the better trump candidate, but indeed affords the *only* way of avoiding loss. On this hand, for example –

♠A K Q J T 9 ♡T 8 6 5 3 2 ♣A ◇—

by all means bid abondance, but nominate hearts as trumps, not the apparently stronger spade suit. The reason is perhaps easiest to see if you examine the hand from the viewpoint of the four losers rather than the nine winners. If you make spades trump, how are you going to avoid losing more than four hearts? With hearts trump, however, you can afford to lose four for the sake of extracting your opponents' trumps and so safely establishing the spade suit. You will make one heart by ruffing a diamond lead, and a second either by a ruff in diamonds or clubs, or by virtue of finding your Ten high when the top trumps have gone.

Defending against an abondance, lead from your longest and strongest suit. Remember that the defenders need five tricks to win, and lose no opportunity to make five as soon as possible – that is, before caller can get in with his trumps and dictate the rest of the play. By all means lead suits in which caller is void, thereby forcing him to trump and so weaken his hand. Sometimes caller will be relying on a 'bum card' for a lucky trick: if you can spot this coming you can defend against it. He may, for instance, lead Ace, King of a side-suit, then switch to another line of attack in pretence of being void. By retaining the odd Queen, Jack or even Ten, instead of discarding at the earliest opportunity, you may well find it winning a low one at the thirteenth trick, led to by caller after extracting all the trumps. Again, if caller is hoping to make a risky King or Queen he may be hoping to do so on a bad lead by the defenders, in which case he will be trying to lose the lead – which you can give him back by forcing him to trump.

Declared abondance. This is a bid to win all thirteen tricks, and as the sort of hand which will enable you to do so is unmistakable there is no point in describing it. Or even playing it; for you only declare abondance on a cast-iron hand, and if it really is cast-iron you simply lay it face up on the table and claim your winnings. If any defender can find a way of beating it then the game must be played, and if he is right you will have learnt a valuable lesson.

It will be worth while explaining why a declared abondance is properly played at no-trump, even though many seem to accept it as a trump game. The reason is, quite simply, that *if* you can make thirteen tricks with a trump suit, then you can make thirteen tricks without a trump suit. 'But surely' (you may say) 'You must declare a trump on a hand with a void, such as –

♠A K Q J T ♡A K Q J ♣A K Q J ◇—

– otherwise, at no-trump, the hand is beaten if diamonds are led.'
Objection overruled. It is precisely to obviate this danger that, for
a declared abondance only, caller has the privilege of leading.

Misère and open misère. Beginners may be forgiven for imagining
that a misère, the winning of no tricks at no-trump, is what you
bid when you have no good trick-winners plus a general
miscellany of dribs and drabs. Such a hand is one on which you
do not bid at all. The misère bid is a positive undertaking
to successfully defend yourself against all efforts on the part of
your opponents to force you to take a trick. For this purpose you
need a very good hand – 'good', that is, from the point of view of
beating off such attacks.

Many card-players, especially those who know nothing but
Bridge, tend to look down on misère as a sort of jocular sub-
stitute round, played when no-one has a good enough hand on
which to make a 'real' bid. Nothing could be further from the
truth. Both attack and defence at misère call for, and often
receive, some of the finest play that can be observed at the card
table.

To business: in contemplating a misère, there are two good
features to look for. One is low-ranking cards, and the other is a
void suit. Note that the length of any suit you hold is irrelevant
so long as it contains low cards. For example, in this hand

♠32 ♡A Q T 8 6 4 2 ♣7 3 2 ◇—

the hearts are just as safe from attack as the spades: you cannot
be forced to take a trick in either suit. As for low ranks, in a
holding of five or more you must have the Two (you may escape
without it, but the risk is great); with fewer, you may get away
with nothing lower than Three or even Four. If your lowest is
the five, you will be beaten if the Four, Three and Two are evenly
distributed among your opponents. Note, too, that a holding of
alternating low ranks is just as good as a sequence. In the hand
quoted above, for instance, the A Q T 8 6 4 2 of hearts is as
strong as would be 8 7 6 5 4 3 2. To prove it, imagine that the
Three is led; you play the Two, and your Four is then the lowest

of the suit. If the Five is then led, you play the Four and your Six is lowest. And so on.

The advantage of a void is obvious: when it is led, you can throw out your potentially dangerous cards. The recognition of potential dangers can be a subtle affair. Take the hand quoted above. Because the hearts are safe from attack, as we have seen, it contains no dangerous cards, so you need not rush to throw out the Ace or Queen when diamonds are led. Clubs, however, are a different matter, for ♣7 is the most dangerous card in the hand. With three clubs, 6, 5, 4, out against you, you can successfully defend against the lead of only two of them (with 3, 2), and by the time the third is led you may find the other two players void, thus forcing you to take with the Seven. (And do not imagine this to be a case of bad luck – experienced opponents will soon discover your weak suit and exploit it.)

You therefore need the void in diamonds as a means of discarding your dangerous Seven. In general, then, you cannot bid misère with dangerous cards unless you have saving voids to accommodate them, and even then the device may only be expected to work once. Remember, too, to look at things from your opponents' viewpoint. If your hand is good enough for a misère but not good enough for an open misère, then by definition it contains a weakness, and the strategy of your opponents will be to find out where this weakness lies and to exploit it. They need to force you to take only one trick to win; once you have done so, the contract is lost and there is no point in playing further.

In defending against a misère a good lead is any singleton, or, failing that, a middling card from a short suit. Do not play from a long suit, as there is a chance that caller will be void and will immediately throw any dangerous card he may hold. Do not play too low, as you must give your partners an opportunity to get rid of their own high cards in that suit. If you hold a Two, especially in a short suit, you may well hold the means to beat the contract. Save it until the top cards are out, then get the lead and play it – for which purpose retain an Ace or other master card to ensure ability to enter when you judge the time ripe.

Sample game

Proposal and acceptance. East deals, and the exposed card is ◇9:

South	♠K 6 5 ♡Q J 8 6 ♣J 2 ◇J T 8 6	
West	♠A J 9 7 2 ♡4 ♣A K 9 6 ◇4 3 2	
North	♠Q T 8 ♡K 9 3 ♣8 7 5 4 3 ◇K Q	
East	♠4 3 ♡A T 7 5 2 ♣Q T ◇A 9 7 5	

South has nothing, and passes. West, taking a calculated risk, proposes, counting a trick for each Ace, one for a ruff on hearts, and hopefully ♣K to boot. North passes. East accepts, on the assumption that his partner has strong trumps (mistakenly) and the other two Aces (correctly). South leads, and having nothing more noteworthy than over a quarter of the trumps available, plunges immediately into that suit.

S	W	N	E	
◇J	◇4	◇Q	◇A	
♡6	♡4	♡3	♡A	Since South seems happy with trumps, East refrains from leading them.
♡8	◇3	♡9	♡2	
♣2	♣K	♣3	♣T	
♣J	♣6	♣4	♣Q	West avoids the Ace – he wants East to take over.
♡J	◇2	♡K	♡2	East, properly, leads into his partner's void. West is now out of trumps, but they need only two tricks.
◇6	♣A	♣5	♠4	Waste of an Ace? Not at all – it draws a trump out.
♡Q	♣9	♣7	♡5	
♠5	♠A	♠8	♠3	
♠6	♣K	♣Q	◇5	
	4		+4	=the required eight tricks

South's trump lead was a danger signal to East: had he continued trumps at the second trick the contract would probably have failed.

Solo. Now it is South's deal, and the turn-up is ♡7:

South ♠K Q 2 ♡A K 7 5 2 ♣K 7 5 4 ◇2
West   ♠T 7 6 ♡Q J 9 6 ♣T 9 6 ◇K Q J
North ♠A J 5 ♡T 8 4 3 ♣A J 8 ◇T 6 4
East   ♠9 8 4 3 ♡— ♣Q 3 2 ◇A 9 8 7 5 3

West, North and East pass, implying sufficient weakness for South to take a solo upon himself, which he accordingly bids. West leads:

S	W	N	E
◇2	◇K	◇4	◇3
♡2	◇Q	♡6	◇5
♡A	♡6	♡3	♠3

South has no side Aces to make and prefers to have his Kings led up to. So he decides to see how the trumps fall, and is aghast to discover East void: if either of the others had five of the other trumps he would be lucky to escape with his life. East throws a spade to conserve his guarded ♣Q and long diamonds.

♠Q	♠6	♠A	♠4

South has no choice but to slip into another suit, aiming to clear a King.

♡K	♡9	♡T	♠8

A nasty lead. Was South's King a mistake or a necessity ? The latter. He must try to make his ♠K.

♠K	♠7	♠5	♠9

Which he now does, for his fourth trick. With four trumps against him in two hands, three of them higher than the Seven, his only chance of another trick lies in the (as yet unseen) club suit. He must force out more trumps to make the clubs safer when they are eventually led. East is void in spades, not so that he can trump (he has none) but because

S	W	N	E	
				the only possible contribution he can make to South's defeat lies either in retaining his guarded Queen or else in leading diamonds.
♡ 5	♡ J	♡ 4	◇ 7	
♡ 7	♡ Q	♡ 8	◇ 8	West leads a trump and the rest fall out. There was no point in retaining the Queen, as South, if he had two trumps, would win anyway.
♠ 2	◇ J	◇ T	◇ A	This looks like the chance that East has been waiting for.
♣ 4	♠ T	♠ J	◇ 9	Better late than never. Now there are three tricks to play, and all players have three clubs in hand. East to lead, and it all depends on him . . .
♣ 5	♣ 6	♣ 8	♣ 2 ?	East has done it wrong!
♣ K	♣ T	♣ J	♣ Q	
♣ 7	♣ 9	♣ A	♣ 3	
5				And South has made his five.

A fascinating deal, victory bestowed with poetic justice. South's bid of solo was perfectly good in theory: a trick for each black King, a ruff on diamonds, and the top two trumps. In practice, the outstanding eight trumps were divided evenly between two opponents, and South should have been beaten by that unfavourable circumstance. And in reality, he made his bid because of a fatal mistake by East at the eleventh hour (or trick, in this case).

It should be obvious to East that South held ♣K. At the eleventh trick East was ideally placed for regicide, lying to the right of the caller. Had he led ♣Q, South could not have played ♣K, for then the Ace would have appeared, leaving him without a fifth trick. He must, therefore, have played low, in which case, East would have kept the trick and retained the lead in precisely the same position; again, South could not have played the King for precisely the same reason, and his Seven would have been taken by anything higher except the Ace, to which the King would fall at the last trick.

This is how the cards lay at the point in question:

South   ♣K 7 5
West   ♣T 9 6
North   ♣A J 8
East   ♣Q 3 2

and it is easy to see that the lead of the Queen is bound to win, whereas anything else is bound to lose.

Misère. West deals, and a club is turned:

South   ♠A J 4 ♡K J ♣J T 8 5 2 ◇Q T 8
West   ♠Q T 9 5 ♡Q 9 6 3 ♣K 9 ◇K 9 2
North   ♠6 3 ♡A T 7 5 2 ♣6 ◇A 7 6 4 3
East   ♠K 8 6 2 ♡8 4 ♣A Q 7 4 3 ◇J 5

North, as eldest, bids misère, and the others pass. This is a shaky bid, marginally justified only by the fact that he has the lead and may get away with his singleton Six at the first trick.

S	W	N	E	
♡5	♣9	♣6	♣4	The fates are kind; and besides, if the opponents had all been able to get under there would have been no tale to tell. West keeps his King of clubs with which to come in later should he get a chance to lead ◇2 or ♡3 with advantage.
♡K	♡6	♡5	♡8	A better lead might have been ◇9.
♡J	♡Q	♡T	♡4	
◇Q	♡9	♡7	◇J	East and South discard from their shortest suits.
◇T	♡3	♡2	◇5	
◇8	◇2	◇7!	♣Q	West, having made a hash of hearts, now leads his winning diamond prematurely. North is right to play high, for he knows that only K, 9, 8 are left in play; if

they lie with West he has lost his
contract anyway, whereas if any of
them lies with South the Seven
must be taken.

| ♠4 | ♠5 | ♠3 | ♠K |
| ♠J | ♠9 | ♠6 | ♠2 |

. . . at which point, North reveals his cards and victory is con-
ceded. This illustrates the sort of misère hand you may get away
with if you are lucky: in fact, as the remaining cards lie, it is not
easy to find a way of beating the contract.

Abondance. North deals, and a heart is turned.

South	♠52	♡AQT52	♣Q9	◇QT75
West	♠74	♡K763	♣86	◇A9862
North	♠AKQJ93	♡—	♣AK432	◇J4
East	♠T86	♡J984	♣JT75	◇K3

Following a prelude of three passes, North bids abondance in
spades. His four losers are to be the two diamonds and two of the
three low clubs, and the main point of his strategy must be to
ensure the win of the third low club. East leads.

S	W	N	E	
◇5	◇2	◇4	◇K	East, having no certain trick, starts to clear his shortest suit and successfully takes his two-to-one chance of winning.
◇7	◇A	◇J	◇3	Good for East; since caller didn't have the Ace, he can lead his Three, void the suit, and ensure the second of the five tricks his side needs to beat the contract.
◇T	◇6	♠J	♡4	A good lead – not that South expects to win the trick, but with so many diamonds gone a possible trump by caller may yet be over-trumped. North is considerably put out by it, and feels obliged to

S	W	N	E	
				trump high. Just as well he did – East is happy to throw a useless card, and could indeed have overtrumped if it had come to the push.
♠2	♠4	♠A	♠6	North must now clear trumps with a view to establishing his clubs.
♠5	♠7	♠K	♠8	
♡2	◇8	♠Q	♠T	That takes care of the last opposing trump. Now North plays from ♠9 3, ♣A K 4 3 2, needing five tricks more.
♣Q	♠6	♣4	♣5	He attacks the club suit from below ...
♡A	♡3	♠3	♡8	... ruffs a long-awaited heart lead, and continues clubs ...
♣9	♠8	♣A	♣7	
◇Q	◇9	♣K	♣T	That leaves the Jack out against his Three and Two.
♡5	♡6	♣3	♣J	
♡T	♡7	♠9	♡9	And in he trumps to lead to the last trick ...
♡Q	♡K	♣2	♡J	... which it is always a joy to win by the lead of a side-suit Two!
		9		Abondance succeeds.

The abondance would not have succeeded if any opponent had held five clubs, which was a risk worth taking. On the assumption that at least one player held four, North made his little club by leading two low ones to force out two high ones, and two high ones to draw out the other two. The whole manoeuvre depended upon his successfully clearing trumps first.

Footnote: In some schools, the caller of an abondance does not announce his trump suit until immediately after the first card has been led to the first trick.

AUCTION SOLO

Auction Solo is substantially the same as basic Solo, but permits a greater degree of competitive bidding, as follows:

> Proposal/acceptance
> 5-trick solo
> 6-trick solo
> 7-trick solo
> 8-trick solo
> Misère
> 9-trick abondance
> 10-trick abondance
> 11-trick abondance
> 12-trick abondance
> Open misère
> No-trump abondance declared
> Trump abondance declared

The 'preferred suit' is established by cutting a second pack rather than by turning up the dealer's last card. Proposal/acceptance and declared abondance in trumps may only be undertaken with the preferred trump. Other solo or abondance bids may be made in any suit, which remains unspecified until the bid has been accepted, but it is possible to overcall any bid by making the same bid in the preferred trump. In other words, the bid 'solo of five' can be overcalled either by 'solo of six' or by 'five in trumps' – meaning in the pre-selected trump.

Different schools vary in which bids they recognise. Proposal/acceptance and a solo of five in one's own suit are often omitted.

In a no-trump abondance declared the bidder leads to the first trick; if there is a trump suit, however, it is made, as usual, by eldest hand.

The value of each game is as follows:

Proposal/acceptance	6, plus 1 per under/over-trick
Solo	6, plus 3 per under/over-trick
Misère	12
Abondance	18, plus 3 per under/over-trick
Open misère	24
Abondance declared	36

If the caller succeeds, he receives the appropriate value from each opponent. (An over-trick is any trick in excess of the number he bid. In some circles, not more than three over-tricks are paid for in a bid of solo, it being argued that the caller should have gone abondance. Settle this point before play.)

If the caller fails, he pays the appropriate value to each opponent. (An under-trick is any trick short of the number he bid – for example, the win of only five tricks in a bid of seven makes two under-tricks.)

Auction Pitch derives from an English game of some antiquity called All Fours, which is described in *The Compleat Gamester* of 1674 as being 'very much play'd in Kent'. Nowadays All Fours and its descendants are little heard of in Britain (except, curiously, in the Blackburn area), but the family as a whole retains a faithful following in America, Mexico, the West Indies, and no doubt other corners of the globe – if a globe may be said to possess corners.

Of the many American varieties that have been devised – California Jack, Seven Up and Cinch are a few of the better known – Auction Pitch strikes me as offering the best balance between chance and skill while still remaining true to the original conception of the game. Though playable by any number from two to seven, it is generally considered best for four.

The All Fours family is probably so called because it attaches importance to four particular features of play – namely, 'high' or highest trump, 'low' or lowest trump, 'Jack', meaning Jack of trumps, and 'game', credited to the player who takes most points in tricks. That the game was well known in the early nineteenth century is indicated by the fact that J. R. Planché, a popular playwright of his time, was able without additional explanation to entitle one of his works 'High, Low, Jack and the Game'.

Auction Pitch may seem trivial at first description, but a few rounds of play are sufficient to uncover subtleties that might not otherwise be expected.

The game

Cards. 52, a standard pack, ranking normally (A K Q J T 9 8 7 6 5 4 3 2).

Game. Game is usually seven points up, lasts for several deals and typically takes 10 to 20 minutes to achieve. It is essentially a gambling game, settlement being made at the end of each game on the basis of scores.

Deal. Six cards to each player, in two batches of three; the others remain face down and out of play.

Object. There is a round of bidding to establish who is to be the pitcher. Pitcher determines the trump suit by leading from it. Tricks are played and the pitcher's object is to score as many points as he bid from amongst the following four features:

1. *High*   1 pt for holding (and therefore winning) the highest trump in play.
2. *Low*   1 pt for capturing, in a trick, the lowest trump in play.
3. *Jack*   1 pt for capturing the Jack of trumps (if in play).
4. *Game*   1 pt for taking in tricks the highest value of scoring cards reckoned on the following basis: any Ace 4, King 3, Queen 2, Jack 1, Ten 10.

(There are 28 cards out of play, so the highest trump in play will not necessarily be the Ace nor the lowest the Deuce. If there is only one trump in play it counts 2, for both highest and lowest, and if it is the Jack it counts 3 for Jack as well. If the Jack is not in play, which happens more often than not, then there are only three game points to be made. Note that although each Ten counts high when scoring for game, it still ranks in normal position between Jack and Nine.)

Bidding. Starting at left of dealer, each player in turn has one chance to bid or pass. The only possible bids are of one, two, three or four, according to the number of scoring features each thinks he can make using his own trump suit. Each succeeding bid must be higher than the previous one. Since four cannot be overbid, a player intending four needn't state it but simply pitches, i.e. leads to the first trick. If all players pass, cards are gathered and the deal moves on.

Tricks. Highest bidder becomes pitcher and leads to the first trick. The suit of the card he pitches, or leads, automatically becomes the trump suit for that round.

When trumps are led players must follow suit if they can. To a non-trump lead, however, each player may either follow suit or trump (even if able to follow), whichever he prefers, but he may not discard from a side-suit. If void in the suit led, a player may either trump or discard from a side-suit.

The trick is won by the highest card of the suit led or by the highest trump if any are played, and the winner of one trick leads to the next.

Score. At the end of play, tricks are examined and whoever has a scoring feature (high, low, Jack, game) scores 1 pt for it. If the Jack was out of play only three game points are available, and if two players tie for game – taking the same value of cards in tricks – then nobody scores the 1 pt for game.

If pitcher has made at least what he bid, he scores what he makes; if not, he is set back by the amount of his bid (hence the alternative name of the game, Setback). Thus, if he bid three and made only two, three is subtracted from his score. A minus score is therefore possible, and is usually indicated by being written with a circle around it.

The winner is the first player to reach or exceed seven points, or whatever total has previously been agreed. All hands are fully played out, and if more than one player including the pitcher goes out on the same hand then pitcher is declared the winner. If more than one goes out but not including the pitcher, then their points are reckoned in order high – low – Jack – game, and the first to have gone out on this basis wins.

Settlement. The winner pays nothing, but receives from the others. As a loser you pay one unit to the winner, plus one unit for each time you were set back during the game, plus one unit if you finished the game in the hole (i.e. with a minus score).

Variants

The point for low. Originally, the point for 'low' went to the player who was dealt the lowest trump in play, regardless of whether he subsequently made or lost it in a trick. It is now customary to score only for capturing the lowest trump in a trick. Players should agree beforehand which version to follow. (It is tempting, but misleading, to assume that more skill is required to capture it from someone else than to know you've got it in the first place.)

Smudge. 'Smudge' is a bid of four made on the understanding that if the bid is successful the bidder scores whatever he needs to win the game. It is therefore particularly useful to a player who is trailing when one or more of the others are close to seven. A player may not bid smudge, however, if he is in the hole; the best he can do from that position is to bid and make all four. There is no extra penalty for failing to make smudge. As a sort of 'double or quits' this variant may be recommended, though it hardly speeds the game up, as four is so rarely bid anyway.

Dealer's overcall. Although in the bidding each new bid must be higher than the preceding one, it may be accepted that dealer can 'relieve' an earlier player of his bid by bidding the same amount. This variant is to be recommended, as it injects a little more variety into the bidding. Note that when this rule is followed, a bid of four can be overtaken by dealer, so an earlier player should merely state 'four' and should not automatically pitch the first card until dealer has passed.

Joker fifth point. A recent development is the addition of a Joker as a fifth point, the usual rule being that it counts below the Two of the trump suit. Whoever captures the Joker in a trick scores 1 pt for it (it does not also count as the lowest trump in play for the purpose of scoring 'low'). If pitcher leads the Joker to the first trick, he states what suit it belongs to for the purpose of establishing trumps, which must of course be followed immediately. With Joker fifth, the highest bid is five, and smudge becomes a pitcher-takes-all bid of five.

Joker fifth is an elaboration that may be disregarded by players who prefer the game to the gambling. Yet further elaborations, such as scoring for the Nine of trumps ('sancho'), the Five of trumps ('pedro'), and others, give rise to virtually new games which are faster but more haphazard than straightforward Auction Pitch.

Hints on play

The play of Auction Pitch hinges almost entirely on trumps. High cards in side-suits are weaker than in most trick-taking games, where there is an obligation to follow suit. Here you may follow suit or trump ad lib. Hence only the pitcher can normally expect to clear out trumps and make with a top card of another colour, for of course pitcher only becomes pitcher by virtue of his strength in trumps. The strategy of his own game will be to clear trumps first – which he is virtually obliged to do in any case because of the requisite trump lead – and to keep forcing them until he is in a position to make good with some side cards. His opponents will correspondingly encourage him to trump tricks that are worth little.

In the bidding, then, the hand must be assessed by reference to its obvious trump suit – only rarely will there be more than one. Length in trumps is better than strength in side-suits. For example, three middling trumps will often produce the point for game, while a side Ace, even singleton, disappears to a trump. Remember that the deal of cards in batches of three instead of one at a time leads to unequal distributions that in any other game would be considered abnormal. In Auction Pitch, a void in the hand is the rule rather than the exception. Indeed, it would be less true to describe a void as a point of strength than to call the absence of a void a positive weakness. A typical hand contains three of one suit and two of another, and if the three includes Ace, King or Queen it is the obvious trump.

Ace of trumps is a certain point for high, Two of trumps only for low if you can be sure of trumping with it and not being over-trumped (assuming you do not play the version in which the point is scored for having been dealt it). To be confident of trumping in with the lowest you must have at least three trumps altogether and preferably four.

There is about a three-in-five chance that your King will be the highest in play or your Three of trumps the lowest; the chance of your Queen being high or your Four low is no better than one in three. If your highest trump is the Jack, you should have it guarded twice to be confident of not losing it to an upper trump. Remember that if you yourself do not hold the scoring Jack there is only a two-in-five chance that it will be in play, and if it is out of play there are only three game points to score. At the other extreme, however, it is theoretically possible to win high, low, Jack *and* game for all four on the strength of a singleton Jack. Possible, but unlikely!

Do not count on making a side Ace unless you have three strong trumps with which to draw the opposition.

It is easy to overreach yourself in the bidding, so do not bid more than you dare especially if you are first or second to call. If dealer is allowed to overcall (recommended) he has a strong position by bidding last, and should not fight shy of taking advantage.

As pitcher, regard the lead of a top trump (Ace, King or Queen) as a general rule to depart from if circumstances seem to warrant it – the strongest circumstance, of course, being the lack of any of those cards. You will obviously never lead the Jack if it is your top trump, and you should even think twice about leading it if you hold a higher card. What happens next depends largely on how players respond to the trump lead. If all show themselves void you are bound to make high, low, and Jack if you have it. An opponent who plays high to a high lead, or drops Jack, Ten or what may well be regarded as the lowest trump, has probably played his last. Anything from Four to Nine may be regarded with suspicion – there is probably another where that came from, and it may be high enough to be dangerous, especially if you hold the Jack. So far as you can without risking the loss of your Jack, Ten (which counts to game) or lowest, you should continue trumps in order to knock as many out as possible. But always be prepared to find three trumps in one opponent's hand, and do not lead Jack or low until you feel them safe.

The most frequent decision that has to be made in play is whether, upon the lead of a side in which you hold a top card, you should follow and take it or disgorge a trump instead. The answer depends on how you estimate the trump holding of the player or two players to follow you: you may be trumped if you follow suit high, or over-trumped if you trump. It is all a matter of judgment.

The extent to which the non-bidders play cooperatively depends much upon the score, for if (as an example) pitcher is trailing and one opponent needs only a single point to game, the latter is only going to be concerned about his single point. Assuming, however, that they are out to beat the pitcher, their best bet is to force him to play second as often as possible – in other words, try to give tricks to the player on pitcher's right. To obviate his point for game, it is also desirable to 'smear', that is, throw high-counting cards (especially Tens) onto one player consistently.

Having the lead, player on dealer's right will do well to lead out nondescript cards from side-suits, especially those in which he holds more rather than fewer cards.

Sample deals

The following deal is worth looking at in some detail. The cards fall thus:

Abel   ♠J 7 6   ♣J   ◇T 4 (*void in* ♡)
Baker   ♠5   ♡T 4 2   ♣K 4 (*void in* ◇)
Charlie   ♡Q 6   ♣7 5   ◇Q 5 (*void in* ♠)
Dealer   ♡K 8 3   ♣Q   ◇A K (*void in* ♠)

Only Dealer has a biddable hand, and after the others pass he bids a possibly cautious 'two', reckoning his King and Three as points for high and low respectively. He duly pitches the King:

A	B	C	D	
♠ 6	♡ 4	♡ 6	♡ K	D assumes there are more trumps about (correctly), and presses the suit in order to clear the way for his probable Three low . . .
♠ 7	♡ T	♡ Q	♡ 8	Now C stands better to make the point for game, but D feels sure he has cleared the hearts.
◇ 4	♠ 5	◇ Q	♡ 3	One for low ?

◇ T	♡ 2!	◇ 5	◇ K	No! The Two *was* in play, and even more points have gone in counting cards towards game. Hardly worth the fussiness of playing King rather than Ace.
♣ J	♣ K	♣ 5	♣ Q	More bad news. The King's in it too.
♠ J	♣ 4	♣ 7	◇ A	
	low		*high*	
	game			
0	2	0	−2	

Dealer has been dogged by bad luck. His Three was undercut, his ♣Q was overpowered, and his three trumps were matched by three in another's hand. As for the counting cards to game, it's as well he didn't reckon on it for a third point.

Or is it? For further examination shows that the game was more than tenable with a different lead – the Eight instead of the King. Like this:

A	B	C	D	
♠ 6	♡ T	♡ Q	♡ 8	
◇ 4	♡ 2	◇ Q	◇ K	Had C led ♡6, a reasonable possibility, D would still win. D avoids trumping here because he needs to conserve his trumps and hopes that someone else will have occasion to trump – as in fact happens, since B, playing last, can be assured of one for low.
♣ J	♣ K	♣ 5	♡ 3	D is safe to trump in low, since it is a well-known fact to all around the table that Abel is void in trumps.
			♡ K	... and D takes the rest.
	low		*high*	
			game	
0	1	0	2	

Having now shown that Dealer did have a bid in hearts, the question on everybody's lips is 'Ought he to know that leading the Eight wins whereas leading the King loses?'.

It is a question that I propose to sidestep altogether by simply pointing out that if he bid on the strength of his two top *diamonds* instead of his trio of miscellaneous hearts, he plays (*a*) ♦A, (*b*) ♦K, (*c*) ♡K and goes on to win three for high, low *and* game!

On the whole, though, I am inclined to believe that his first pitch was proper, even though it lost.

Here is another interesting situation:

Abel   ♠A ♡3 ♣J 8 6 2 (*void in* ♦)
Baker   ♠6 ♡Q T 9 ♣9 ♦8
Charlie ♠9 8 ♡5 ♣A ♦9 2
Dealer ♠K T ♡3 ♣K T 5 (*void in* ♦)

Only the players with voids have biddable hands. Baker and Charlie pass (note how an absence of voids is a weakness), and Dealer bids two with an eye to his clubs. Abel thereupon bids three with an eye to *his* clubs, and pitches the Eight:

A	B	C	D	
♣8	♣9	♣A!	♣5	Dealer is surprised to find his suit pitched, and both he and Abel are even more surprised to see the Ace turned up.
♠A	♠6	♠9	♠K	Dealer might have trumped, but he doesn't wish to give ten away, and the King may be used to catch something valuable.
♦3	♦8	♦9	♣T	Now he trumps in order to lead through Abel.
♣2	♡9	♡5	♡3	A miscellaneous lead, and pointless in the event, though Abel was taking a chance on playing the lowest trump with two other players to follow. However, he is

now lulled into a false sense of
security, and decides that it must
now be safe to lead the Jack.

| ♣ J | ♡ Q | ◇ 2 | ♣ K! | Which it isn't. |
| ♣ 6 | ♡ T | ♠ 8 | ♠ T | The two Tens fail to compensate ... |

| *low* | | *high* | *Jack* |
game			
−3	0	1	1

Abel ought to have acted on the assumption that someone else
could take the Jack, and ought, therefore, to have played his last
two cards the other way round. Had he done so, he would have
made his bid.

11

SEVEN-CARD RUMMY
A game of melds

There are so many versions of Rummy that the name hardly serves to distinguish any one of them. Two of the most successful fad games of the century, Gin and Canasta, though superficially distinct from each other are members of the same Rummy family, and are based on features common to them all.

The object of any Rummy is to collect matched sets of cards called 'melds', and to 'go out' by melding all the cards you hold. A meld may consist of three or more cards of the same rank, or of three or more cards of the same suit and in numerical sequence. The means by which the object is achieved is that of constant card-exchange through the 'stock' and 'discard' piles. At each turn a player draws either the face-down card of the stock or the face-up card of the discard pile, adds it to his hand, makes any melds he can, and plays a card out to the discard pile. The point of the game is to note what others are discarding and to modify your own strategy according to the information so gained.

There are countless variations on this basic theme, none of which obscures it from view. The game described in this chapter presents it in one of its simplest and most uncluttered forms, and is the game that most players mean when they intend to play 'Rummy' without specifying which one. Though not specifically designed for four, being comfortably playable by any number (doubling the pack where necessary), in practice four may be said to give the game its finest balance. It serves as a good introduction to all members of the family. In particular, no-one ought properly to embark upon Canasta without prior experience of this forerunner.

Rummy, also known as Rum and probably named after the alcoholic beverage, is an historically new game, barely a hundred years old. The family seems to have developed in the southern American states from a Mexican game called Con Quian, Americanised to Coon Can. An alternative theory, to the effect that Con Quian derives from Coon Can (instead of vice versa), and that Rummy derives ultimately from Poker, is open to continued debate.

The game

Cards. A standard 52-card pack.

Game. A game may consist of any agreed number of deals, preferably a multiple of four, or be played up to a previously agreed total of points – say 100 for a short game, 500 for a long one.

Deal. Determine who is to deal first by any agreed means; thereafter, the turn to deal and all play pass clockwise around the table. Shuffle the cards thoroughly before each deal. Deal seven cards each, one card at a time and face down. Place the remainder face down in a squared-up pile forming the *stock* in the middle of the table, then turn the top card and lay it face up beside the stock to start the *discard pile*, which must also be kept squared up as it grows during the course of the game. The top, face-up card of the discard pile at any point in the game is known as the upcard.

Object. The object of the game is to be the first player to 'go out' by getting rid of all the cards in your hand. During the game you exchange cards in your hand for cards from the stock and discard piles, but you can only get rid of them in groups of three or more matching sets called melds, or by subsequently adding individual cards to melds already visible on the table. The first player to go out scores the total value of all the cards remaining in his opponents' hands. Since unmelded cards – known as 'deadwood' – count against you if someone else goes out first, a secondary objective is to reduce the amount of deadwood likely to count against you in this eventuality, by swapping high-valued cards for those of low value even if they do not belong to meldable combinations.

Rank and value of cards and melds. Cards run in the following order: K Q J T 9 8 7 6 5 4 3 2 A. A meld consists of three or more cards of the same rank (e.g. three or four Kings, Twos, Aces etc.) or three or more cards of the same suit and in numerical order (e.g. ♠K Q J etc. or ♡A 2 3 etc. or ♣T 9 8 etc. Note that the Ace is always low, and is not in immediate sequence with the King). The penalty value of unmelded cards at the end of the game is their face value, i.e. Ace, 1, Two, 2 etc., with face cards counting ten each.

Play. Starting with the player on the dealer's left, each in turn (*a*) must *draw*, (*b*) may *meld*, then (*c*) must *discard* (if possible), in that order.

Draw. You must first draw either the top (face-down) card of the stock, or the upcard, and add it to your hand.

Meld. You may then, if you can and if you wish, make one or more melds and/or 'lay off' any card or cards from your hand that match existing melds on the table.

Any new meld you make must consist of at least three cards of the same rank or sequence, and you meld it by laying it face up on the table before you, with the cards slightly spread so that all are visible.

You may lay off a single card against any existing meld of your own *or* of any of your opponents, so long as it properly matches. (*Example:* you could lay off ◇6 against a meld consisting of ♠6 ♡6 ♣6, or against a sequence such as ◇3 4 5 or ◇9 8 7.)

You are not *obliged* to meld or lay off when you can: the skill of the game lies in knowing when to do so and when to refrain.

Discard. Whether you have melded or not, you must finish your turn by discarding any card face up to the discard pile, unless, of course, you have just won by melding the last card(s) in your hand. You also win if the card you discard was the last left in your hand.

Continuation. Play proceeds in this way and ends as soon as one player goes out. If no-one has done so by the time the stock runs out, the following procedure applies. The player who drew the last card of the stock discards in the usual way. The next player in turn may, if he wishes, turn the discard pile upside down (without shuffling) to form a new stock and must then draw the top card from it, or else draw the upcard and make his discard in the usual way, in which case the next player in turn has the same option.

Score. The player who goes out scores the total face value of all cards left in his opponents' hands, regardless of whether or not any of them can be melded or laid off. If he goes out in a single turn, getting rid of all seven cards without having previously made a meld or lay-off, his score is doubled. (This is known as 'going rummy'.)

Irregularities. Most irregularities can be settled by agreement and common sense, as in all card games, but one is worth noting in particular. If a player accidentally draws two cards from the stock, he must keep the top one (which he should have drawn singly) and replace the other face *up* on the stock pile. This, of course, gives the player on his left the choice of two visible cards at his turn to play.

Hints on play

Although its best friend could hardly call Rummy an intellectually stimulating game, it probably calls for more skill than many card-players give it credit for, the skills required being those of alertness, observation, and common sense. Although Rummy is a game of chance in the short term, experienced players will never-theless consistently win in the long run, so it is reasonable to ask how they do it.

Perhaps the most fundamental type of skill born of experience is the one most difficult to analyse and convey: it can probably best be described as intuition. In practice it means that you make melds and lay off cards when there is an imminent danger that an opponent will go out, in order to reduce the amount of deadwood scoring against you, but refrain from doing so when you feel that there is no such danger.

The advantage of not melding immediately is that it reduces

the opportunity for opponents to lay off individual cards against your melds, while retaining for yourself the profitable possibility of building up melds and individual matching cards with a view to going rummy – i.e. getting rid of all seven cards in one turn.

Another advantage is that it gives the others no clear indication of how close you are to going out, and it is because the others will probably be following the same procedure (for the same reason) that you will have little information on which to judge how well they are doing. Naturally, any player who makes early melds and has few cards left in hand represents a danger, and what often happens is that all players retain their seven cards until one of them cracks under the strain and makes a meld, whereupon the others follow suit in order to reduce their deadwood.

Some indication of your opponents' progress may be gleaned from observing how they play. The person who plays slowly and thoughtfully, drawing frequently from the discard pile, usually has a wildly assorted hand and is doing his best to improve it by making part-melds and reducing deadwood – the latter is particularly noticeable if he draws upcards of low face value and discards those of higher count. On the other hand, the player who seems to be drawing solely from stock and ignoring the upcard may well be desperately searching for one particular card that will complete his hand and enable him to meld himself out. He, therefore, is the one to watch.

It goes without saying that you can form some idea of what players are collecting by noting the upcards they take (especially if they are foolish enough to transfer openly to the discard pile the card they have just drawn from stock); what they are not collecting can be deduced by observing their discards. What you can actually do with this information is somewhat limited, and of a negative kind; for example, if you need a particular card for a potential meld, and see it discarded by anyone other than the player on your right, you will have to give up that combination and start working on something else.

Sensible play on your own part lies in preferring to throw out isolated and high-scoring cards in exchange for matching and low-scoring ones. Build up part-melds until they become full melds, but give them up when you see cards you need discarded by others and rendered inaccessible to you. In following this procedure there will inevitably come a point at which the only discard you can make must be from a part-meld. Suppose, for example, you hold ♠5 3, ♡5 4, ♣Q 6, ◇Q, and you draw from stock ♣4. This belongs to the same sequence as ♣6, also matches ♡4, and forces you to discard from a potential combination. Which to break up depends, of course, on what other cards you may have seen in play – for example, the Queens are hardly worth retaining if you know that a third is buried in the discard pile, or if it is visible on the table as part of a sequence meld, and it would be as well to start discarding them for the sake of lowering the total face value of cards in hand. But none of this would apply if the hand illustrated were the one dealt to you, and ♣4 were the first card drawn. In this particular case it would be best to discard ♣6. For one thing, the hand is naturally falling into melds of rank rather than sequences; for another, the sequences you do hold (♠5 3 and ♣6 4) run across gaps. Thus the ♠5 3 sequence can only be completed by the draw of one card, the Four, whereas a two-card sequence such as ♠4 3 could be filled by either the Five or the Two. Similarly, each of the pairs you hold (Queens, Fives and Fours) can be completed by the addition of either of two cards – a much better bet than either of the two gapped sequences. So either the ♠3 or the ♣6 must go. Of the two, the Six is very marginally better on principle, being of higher value.

Generally, draw the upcard if it looks even remotely useful. If it later proves not to be, you can always discard it again, but there could be nothing more frustrating than rejecting an upcard which, within a few more turns, would have turned out to be extremely profitable. This principle applies with greatest force at the beginning of the game, or at any time when you hold a highly varied hand. When, of course, you reach a point at which your probable melds are firmly set you will prefer to draw from the stock pile in the hope of finding particular cards you want.

Never draw a card from stock and play it immediately to the discard pile. For one thing, it gives too much of your game away to your opponents. For another, the very sloppiness of the action will prevent you from thinking carefully about your hand and perhaps making a wiser move. Every time you draw from stock, add it to your hand and consider it anew, for you now have eight cards instead of seven, and they may fall into new combinations.

Sample game

At each turn, we will give the player's complete hand so that his draw and discard may be seen in context. When a player is said to 'draw' a card, the draw is made from the stock (the card unseen); when he is said to 'take' it, this means that he takes the upcard, i.e. the card discarded face up by the previous player. The verbal distinction is made purely for convenience here; it is not a customary form of terminology.

South   ♠K 3 ♡K 8 4 ◇7 5

The upcard is ◇2, which bears no relation to the hand as dealt. South accordingly draws from stock ♠A, which is at least in range with ♠3, and rejects ♡8 as being unrelated to anything else in this regrettably miscellaneous opening hand.

West   ♠6 ♡Q T 3 ♣J 3 ◇8

With a pair of Threes and little else of any use, West ignores the upcard and draws ♡8. This is good: it matches ◇8 and is only a gap away from ♡T should a heart sequence materialise. He discards ♠6, and might have done better to discard the Jack.

North   ♠7 ♡9 6 ♣7 2 ◇J T

North takes the ♠6, as it lies in sequence with ♠7 and forms a second pair with ♡6. The obvious discard is ♡9.

East   ♠9 8 ♡7 ♣4 ◇Q 9 4

No hesitation in taking ♡9, as it gives him three Nines. East could now meld, but there is no hurry: with three Nines and a pair of Fours after a single turn he can at least think about going rummy. He discards ◇Q.

South   ♠K 3 A ♡K 4 ◇7 5

The Queen being unhelpful, South draws ♡2 – which is equally unhelpful, and consequently discarded.

West ♡Q T 8 3 ♣J 3 ◇8

This suits West, who takes the ♡2 and banishes ♣J from his hand.

North ♠7 6 ♡6 ♣7 2 ◇J T

North takes ♣J and discards ◇T, perhaps surprisingly, as ♣2 seems the more likely candidate. Certainly ♣J is a better companion for ◇J than ◇T, since ◇Q has been discarded and there is only one way of filling the sequence (namely ◇9) as opposed to two ways of completing the Jacks (♠J, ♡J); but retaining the Ten as well would have given North three opportunities of using ◇J in a meld. Possibly North was merely discarding a high count on principle.

East ♠9 8 ♡9 7 ♣4 ◇9 4

Draws ♣8 and discards ♡7. The Eight matches ♠8, whereas the Seven matches nothing (not even ♡9, which, besides being a gap away, is otherwise engaged).

South ♠K 3 A ♡K ♣A ◇7 5

Takes ♡7, discards ♠3. There is little point in relating ♠3 to ♠A for a sequence, as there is a gap in the middle and the Ace is more likely to perform in conjunction with ♣A.

West ♡T 8 4 3 2 ♣3 ◇8

A difficult decision: the ♠3 upcard gives him a meld of Threes, but breaks up the heart sequence, leaving ♡2 useless. Still, a bird in the hand is better than two in the stockpile, so West takes the black Three and discards ♡T (as ♡9 has already been seen and taken; that sequence is pointless anyway).

North ♠7 6 ♡6 ♣J 7 2 ◇J

There is nothing to be gained from the Ten, so North draws from stock and is pleased to find ◇6, giving him three of a kind.

He has no urgency to meld, and completes his turn by discarding the only completely non-matching card in his hand, ♣2.

East ♠98 ♡9 ♣84 ◇94

To this promising hand of a trio and two pairs, East draws ♡5 from stock, and, after feigning careful consideration of the possibilities, discards it again.

South ♠K A ♡K 7 ♣A ◇75

With three pairs and an idler, South sees nothing to be gained by swapping a Seven for a Five and therefore draws from stock ♠T, which he promptly – but not too obviously – transfers to the discard pile.

West ♠3 ♡8432 ♣3 ◇8

West draws ◇3 and could hardly be more pleased, for it gives him the Threes without loss of the sequence. Should he now meld? If he does not, he may be caught out, but if he does, he loses the possibility of matching his last card and going rummy. But this is no loss, since there are no more Threes and the other cards of the sequence have been seen in the discards (♡5 and ♡A are gone). He therefore melds his sequence and his Threes, and discards ♡8, leaving the other Eight in hand. His hope is that others will now meld, and perhaps thereby give him the opportunity of laying off his last card to one of their sets.

North ♠76 ♡6 ♣J7 ◇J6

A good-looking hand, but improved neither by the upcard nor by the ◇K, which he now draws from stock. He melds his three Sixes and discards the said King.

East ♠98 ♡9 ♣84 ◇94

Another promising hand. East draws from stock and finds himself luckier than North in acquiring ♠4. He melds his Nines and Fours, retains ♣8 and discards ♠8.

South ♠K A ♡K 7 ♣A ◇75

Opponents are melding right, left and centre, and poor South has nothing useful yet. Fortunately, he draws ♣K, which he promptly melds with his others, discarding ◇5.

West   ◇ 8

West draws ♠Q, and unceremoniously scraps it.

North   ♠7 ♣J 7 ◇J

He draws ♠2, and discards it.

East   ♣ 8

Draws ♣T, and discards it. Subtlety has ceased to have any survival value.

South   ♠A ♡7 ♣A ◇7

Draws ◇A – another turn-up for the book. He refrains from melding the Aces, for fear that someone else should go out by laying off the fourth – though, if his memory served him better, he would recall that ♡A was discarded a long time ago. But to avoid melding is a not-unreasonable little bluff, since the Aces would only count three against if put to the test. South discards ♡7 and keeps mum.

West   ◇8

Draws ♡J; discards ♡J.

North   ♠7 ♣J 7 ◇J

North takes the available Jack and ought now to meld the trio, but does not. To some extent he is following the same argument as South, since the more melds are made available on the table the more chance there is for others to meld themselves out by laying cards off to them. South, however, had only Aces in hand, counting 1 each; North has Jacks, which are a good deal more. He discards ♠7.

East   ♣ 8

Draws ♣Q, and discards it.

South ♠A ♣A ♢A 7

Draws ♣6, melds three Aces, lays the Six off to East's meld of Sixes, discards ♢7, and goes out.

South therefore wins, and scores from each player as follows:

West   8 (♢8)
North   37 (♣7 and three Jacks)
East   8 (♣8)
Total   53

Had North been sensible enough to meld his Jacks, South's score would have been reduced by 30.

This game well illustrates the problem of melding down to one card, as West did when he made the first meld of the game. This move ought not to have provoked the others into melding, for doing so only gave West opportunities of getting rid of his last card (the fact that he did not actually go out does not alter the principle involved). It was quite clear to the others that West could not meld himself out so long as they left him nothing to which he could lay off, since his own melds (♡4 3 2 and three Threes) could not be completed until the stock was turned, and then only if he drew ♡5 or ♡A.

Variants

An alternative scoring system is for the player who goes out to count nothing, and for each other to count the value of his cards as a penalty score. Thus in the game above South would have scored 0, West and East 8 each, and North 37. The winner is then the player who has the lowest score when one player reaches a previously agreed penalty target – say 50. This system produces less extreme results, and may be preferred for that reason.

Knock Rummy

In this version the basic mechanics are the same and the object, as before, is to collect melds and reduce deadwood. The difference, however, lies in the fact that melds are kept in hand and not revealed on the table.

Play proceeds until one player is satisfied with the hand he has collected and ends the game by knocking on the table, which he must do after drawing a card but before discarding. All players then reveal their hands, separating melds from deadwood, and the winner is the player with the lowest deadwood count.

If the knocker has the lowest count, he scores from each other player the difference in count between his deadwood and theirs. If he has no deadwood, he scores a bonus of 25 per opponent, even if another has none either.

If a player ties with the knocker for lowest count, the tying player wins instead and scores as described above.

If the knocker does not have the lowest count, all those with lower counts than the knocker score 10 from him, and the player with the lowest collects from the others as described above.

There are many other variants of Rummy. Five Hundred Rum, which is detailed in *Teach Yourself Card Games for Three*, may also be played by four.

12 THREE GAMES OF REVERSE
Domino Hearts—Slobberhannes—Bassadewitz

There is a large family of games in which, although tricks are played 'in the normal way' (see page 7), the object is not to win tricks but either to avoid winning them, or more usually, to avoid winning specific penalty cards which they may contain. One such ancestral game was called Reversis, since the object was regarded as being the reverse of normal trick-playing procedure, and it would be convenient and proper to group them together under the heading 'Reverse family'. Because the Reverse games best known to English and American card-players are those in which the penalty cards are always hearts, the term 'Hearts family' is more generally used.

Only one of the Reverse games grouped together in this chapter features hearts as the penalty to be avoided, though four players may also play Black Maria, which is described in *Teach Yourself Card Games for Three*. Domino Hearts starts off like the Block Game at dominoes, whence its name, but soon reaches a point at which the play is exactly like that at Black Maria. Slobberhannes, though little played, is a far more subtle game than its bald description might suggest, and is worthy of revival. Bassadewitz, for whose inclusion I make no apology, is (or was) an obscure nineteenth-century German game which will be of interest to players of Skat, Pinochle or versions of Jass.

They are grouped together partly because they follow much the same principles and call for similar skills, and partly because none of them merits in-depth treatment on its own.

Domino Hearts

Cards. A standard 52-card pack.

Deal. Deal six cards each, one at a time, and place the remainder of the pack face down to one side of the table to form a stock.

Object. The ultimate object of the game is to avoid taking any tricks containing hearts, though sometimes little may be done towards this end until the undealt stock of cards is exhausted.

Play: first half. There are no trumps. The player to the dealer's left leads to the first trick, and others must follow suit. The trick is won by the person who played the highest card of the suit led, and he then leads to the next trick. If you are unable to follow suit to the card led you may not play anything else, but must instead draw cards from the top of the stock and add them to your hand until you can follow suit. If you run out of cards before the stock is exhausted you stop playing for the rest of the deal while the others continue in the normal way. This continues until the stock is exhausted.

Play: second half. As soon as the last card of the stock has been drawn, the rules of play change. If now any player is unable to follow suit to the card led, he may discard anything from his hand. As soon as a player plays his last card, he drops out. (If he won a trick with it, the next lead is made by the player on his left.) When only one player has any cards left, he adds them to his won tricks and play ceases.

Score. Each player scores a penalty of 1 pt for every heart he has taken. The winner is the player with the lowest score after a previously agreed number of deals (which should be a multiple of four), or with the lowest score as soon as one player reaches a previously agreed penalty total, such as 30 for a game of reasonable length.

If a plus score is preferred, each player scores the total number of hearts taken by his three opponents (or, which comes to the same thing, thirteen minus the number he has taken himself). In this case the winner is the first player to reach or exceed a score of (say) 30.

Hints on play

The situation when the stock is exhausted is exactly like that of other Hearts games, except that players do not necessarily hold the same number of cards, and the same principles of play therefore apply.

Your chief concern is to avoid taking hearts – 'clean' tricks, containing none of them, are perfectly safe. With several low hearts (having regard to those that have been taken during the first half of the game), it is good practice to lead them out, as others will be forced to take, and there will be few if any left for tricks you may have to win later with high cards in other suits. With only high hearts, your only chance to avoid being forced to win with them is to have the opportunity of throwing them to leads of suits in which you are void; therefore, your chief concern will be to create voids in other suits. Do this by leading them if it appears safe to do so – that is, if there is little danger of others' throwing hearts to them, and by throwing them to other suit leads in which you may also be void. This point had better be illustrated. Suppose, for example, you hold

$$\heartsuit 5 \quad \clubsuit K \quad \diamondsuit — \quad \spadesuit Q\,4\,2$$

and diamonds are led; here it would be safer to throw the $\clubsuit$K than the $\heartsuit$5, as you thereby create two voids and get rid of a dangerous card with which you might later be forced to take a trick containing penalty cards. It is unnecessary to throw the $\heartsuit$5, as it is sufficiently low to be unlikely to take a heart trick. Nor need you worry about the $\spadesuit$Q, for, holding the Four and the Two, you can expect to escape from taking a trick on two leads of spades, and by the time these have gone you will almost certainly have had an opportunity to discard the Queen to a lead in one of your voids.

Again, given the lead from the above hand, play $\heartsuit$5. This can only be a liability in the unlikely event that the three lower cards are distributed one each amongst your opponents, even assuming they have not been played out during the first half of the game.

There is one feature in which the game differs from normal Hearts, and this is that players have hands of unequal lengths in the second part of the game. If, therefore, you hold the longest hand, you must avoid a situation in which others go out and leave you with unplayed hearts to add to your tricks at the end of the game. With a long hand, lose no opportunity to get rid of hearts.

What happens in the first half of the game is to a large extent a matter of chance, depending much upon what cards you have to draw before being able to follow suit. You therefore have little control over the holding of cards with which you enter the second half.

Having to draw cards from the stock when unable to follow suit can be advantageous, especially if your holding of hearts lacks low ranks with which to avoid being forced to take. If you do have low ones, hearts are very good to lead in the first half, as anyone who is void will have to draw until they can follow suit and is therefore unlikely to be able to leave you holding the baby (or, more precisely, holding the trick with a low card).

Generally, however, you would prefer not to draw – in fact, the objective of escaping play by getting rid of all your cards in the first half of the game would be a good one to aim for, if only the mechanics of the game enabled you to exert sufficient control over the process. Try to force others to draw as often as possible by leading from your longest suit (on the assumption that they are likely to be deficient in it), and – except in hearts, of course – play high to win as often as possible, in order to be able to dictate the suit of the next trick. But when the stock is near its end lead low, in case a player void in the suit exhausts the stock without finding any and starts throwing hearts.

Sample deal

South	♡5 4	♣8	◇T 5	♠9
West	♡T	♣K	◇9 7	♠K T
North	♡J 8	♣9 4	◇K 2	♠—
East	♡Q 7	♣2	◇Q	♠J 8

S	W	N	E	
♡ 5	♡ T	♡ 8	♡ 7	South can afford to open aggressively.
♠ 9	♠ K	♠ Q	♠ J	North, void in spades, drew ♣A, ♡3, ♠Q before playing.
♠ 4	♠ T	♠ A	♠ 8	West drew ◇4, ♠4; South drew ♣7, ♠4.
♣ 8	♣ K	♣ A	♣ 2	
◇ 5	◇ 9	◇ K	◇ Q	
♣ 7	♣ Q	♣ 9	♣ 5	North drew ♡A, ♠6; East drew ♣5.
♠ 2	♠ 6	♠ 5	♠ 7	A profitable suit lead from West, the others having to draw cards with the following results: North ♣T, ◇A, ♣3, ♡6, ♠5; East ♡9, ♣6, ♣J, ◇J, ◇8, ♡2, ♠7; South ♠2.
◇ T	◇ 7	◇ A	◇ J	
◇ 6	♡ A	◇ 4	♡ 8	A bad lead from East – he should have watched the stock and led low. South drew ♡K, ♠3, ◇6; West drew the last card, which was ♡A, and thereby entitled himself to throw it to the trick. Now he is out of cards and play.
	out			

At the start of the second half, only three players are left in; their hands are as follows:

    South   ♡K 4 ♠3
    North   ♡J 6 3 ♣T 4 3 ◇3 2
    East   ♡Q 9 2 ♣J 6

Although North appears to lie at a disadvantage in holding the most cards, they are comparatively safe ones – he is unlikely to be forced into taking a trick, and need concentrate only on throwing out the hearts before his opponents run out of cards altogether. And he will be more than happy with a heart lead. It is now East to lead:

S	W	N	E	
♡K	—	♣4	♣6	Unlucky or ill-judged ? East did not want to lead his only safe heart, preferring to retain the Two in order to escape from a heart lead; knowing the highest club in play to be the Ten, he hoped to have his Six overtaken.
♡4	—	♡3	♡2	Now the Two is his only hope.
♠3	—	♡J	♡Q	An unhappy last trick for South, who is now out of cards. The lead therefore passes to the next active player on his left, who is North.
—	—	♣T	♣J	
		♡6	♡9	
5	4	0	4	penalty cards (hearts) taken
8	9	13	9	score by plus-score system

It will be noted that West, in the event, gained nothing by going out first, and that North, though lumbered with the longest hand at the start of the second half, succeeded in avoiding all penalties.

Slobberhannes

This refined little game belies the grossness of its unexplained low-Germanic title – which indeed may have been responsible for its eclipse. It is similar to, but in my view finer than, the game of Polignac, which is blessed with a more civilised-sounding name.

Cards. A 32-card Piquet pack (i.e. lacking all Sixes and lower ranks).

Deal. Cut the pack to determine who is to lead to the first trick. This privilege goes to the player cutting the highest card (Ace counting high). The cards are then shuffled and dealt, one at a time, by the player to the leader's right, each player receiving eight.

Object. To avoid winning the first trick, the last trick, and the trick containing ♣Q.

Play. Cards rank in their usual order, from high to low: A K Q J T 9 8 7. There are no trumps, and the normal rules of trick-taking apply: follow suit to the card led if possible; if not, play any card. The trick is taken by the highest card of the suit led, and the winner of a trick leads to the next.

Score. There is a penalty of one point each for taking the first trick, the last trick and the ♣Q, and an additional penalty point if one player takes all three (he therefore counts four instead of three).

Revoke. It is customary to count one penalty point for revoking (failing to follow suit though able to do so).

Hints on play

The play revolves entirely around the three penalty features, and winning or losing tricks in itself is meaningless except in assisting you to avoid them. It is vital to observe how opponents are playing and to remember the cards that have gone, for although your play to many tricks may be forced, there are few games in which so much may hinge on making the correct choice of play when the occasion arises.

Unless you have exceptionally bad cards, or the cards are exceptionally badly distributed, it is easy to avoid winning the first trick when you have the lead. Anything lower than Ten will almost certainly lose: the lead of a Nine, for example, can only fail if one opponent is void in the suit and the Eight and Seven lie between the other two instead of in one hand. The lead of a Ten, if you hold nothing lower, will only lose if the Nine, Eight and Seven are evenly distributed amongst the other players: the chances are five to two in your favour.

In defensive play against the ♣Q penalty, the penalty card itself as well as ♣K and ♣A are dangerous to hold and must be got rid of unless adequately guarded. If you hold one of these cards and a lower club you are probably safe, and more certainly so if you hold two lower. If you hold low clubs only the suit may safely be led; in fact you should lead them, to avoid being left with possibly winning clubs towards the last trick after the dangerous cards have been thrown. If you hold high clubs only your sole chance of losing them is to tricks led in suits of which you have none, for which purpose, of course, it is desirable to create voids where you can.

Avoidance of the last trick is effected by playing high during the course of the game and retaining low cards for the end play. Much of the excitement of the game derives from the clash that may arise in pursuit of these objectives: the danger of playing high cards in mid-game to avoid taking the last trick with any of them lies in the possibility that opponents will void themselves in the suit you are leading and so spring the black Queen upon you. This is why so much depends on close observation of what the others are playing.

Sample game

South cuts highest and acquires the lead, and East deals, with the following result:

South	♣J T	◇T 9	♠K J	♡K T
West	♣K 8	◇J	♠Q T 9	♡9 8
North	♣A 9	◇K Q 7	♠8	♡A 7
East	♣Q 7	◇A 8	♠A 7	♡Q J

A very even distribution. South has middling cards and may have difficulty in losing the last trick, though he seems safe in clubs. Each of his opponents has a high club once guarded, and can therefore play with a view to avoiding the penalty.

1st trick

South	◇ T
West	◇ J
North	◇ 7
East	◇ 8

South leads the safest of his middling cards. He might, for fun, have led clubs and rendered the Queen penalty imminent; but although there is only a two-in-seven chance that the three lower clubs are evenly distributed in general theory, in actual practice his own holding is so evenly distributed (two of each suit) as to suggest that the two against might prove to be more probable than the five for. And, in the event, he is right.

West had no option but to take the trick, but as consolation for his singleton Jack he now has a void suit through which his ♣K may be led to safety.

2nd trick
West   ♠ Q
North   ♠ 8
East   ♠ A
South   ♠ K

West could lead a heart with a view to a second void, or the high spade with a view to retaining low cards for the end play; he chooses the latter.

3rd trick
East   ♦ A
South   ♦ 9
West   ♣ K
North   ♦ Q

East faces problems with his lead. Clubs are not on; diamonds have gone one round, and if he leads the Ace he could possibly draw both ♣A and ♣K, leaving his Queen high; and to lead his best card, ♠7, may leave him with the last trick.

He chooses the ♦A, which is good for West as it enables him to offload his dangerous King, and good for North, as the ♦K with which he is left is now the only diamond in play and hence is no liability for the last trick (unless, of course, he wins the penultimate trick and is forced to lead it).

4th trick
East   ♡ Q
South   ♡ K
West   ♡ 9
North   ♡ A

This lead suits everybody.

> 5th trick
> North   ♡ 7
> East   ♡ J
> South   ♡ T
> West   ♡ 8

All these cards, including the lead, are singletons and therefore forced. North would obviously not lead ◇K — it being the only diamond in play, the holder of ♣Q would throw it to him immediately. The same would happen on the lead of ♣A; and the lead of ♣9 would certainly give him the last trick.

> 6th trick
> East   ♠ 7
> South   ♠ J
> West   ♠ T
> North   ♣ A

East's lead is obvious. South and West have no choice; North is pleased to lose his Ace. But the only small consolation for East, whose Queen is now high, lies in the fact that he is playing last to the next trick and can therefore make his choice of play in full knowledge of the consequences.

> 7th trick
> South   ♣ J
> West   ♣ 8
> North   ♣ 9
> East   ♣ Q!

East is forced to take the trick with his own penalty card. Knowing the only other club in play to be the Ten, he can see that if it lies with South, and he throws the Seven, South's next lead of ♣T will give him (East) the Queen *and* the last trick for two penalties. By taking the Queen himself, East can lead ♣7 in the knowledge that it will be taken by Ten.

Why, it may be asked, does he act on the assumption that ♣T lies with South, and not with West or North, in which case East could have played the Seven and avoided both penalties? Is he not accepting a certain penalty point in exchange for a two-in-three chance of escaping the double penalty?

The answer is that East is either a brilliant player or has been taking notes surreptitiously under the table. The outstanding cards are ♣T, ◇K and ♠9, West has shown himself void in diamonds (*3rd trick*), and North in spades (*6th trick*). So the three possibilities of distribution are: South ♣, West ♠, North ◇ (the unfavourable distribution), or South ♠, West ♣, North ◇, or South ◇, West ♠, North ♣. Now, the third possibility is unlikely, as South would surely have played ◇K to the *3rd trick* instead of the Nine; and if West had held ♣T, he would in the present trick surely have played it in preference to the Eight, having seen the Jack but not the Nine (which came after him, from North).

East therefore takes the risk, and is justified by the result of the . . .

7th trick

East	♣ 7
South	♣ T!
West	♠ 9
North	◇ K

Thus South, North and East score one penalty apiece for last, first and Queen respectively, and North emerges with a clean sheet.

Bassadewitz

There is a large group of games, of central European origin, in which tricks are of no value in themselves but only for the scoring cards, or 'counters', which they may contain. The counting cards are, typically, Ace 11, Ten 10, King 4, Queen 3, and Jack 2, making a total of 30 points to be won in each suit, or 120 in the whole pack. Many fine games, including Skat and Pinochle, belong to this family, to which Klaverjass (see p. 65) is also related.

Bassadewitz is a 'reverse' member of it: the object is to score as few points as possible by the capture of counting cards – in other words, to try to avoid taking them. The name is pronounced with the stress on the second syllable, and the W like a V; an alternative version of the name is Bassarowitz, and I have no idea as to the origin of either. The game is taken from a book published in 1888 called *German and French Games at Cards*, by a man who wrote under the name Aquarius in order to hide his real name, which was, in fact, Jackson – Louis d'Aguilar Jackson, to do him justice.

The game

Cards. A 32-card Piquet pack (no Sixes or lower ranks).

Deal. Deal cards two at a time, face down, until each player has eight.

Object. Tricks are played at no-trump and the object is to avoid taking points in counting-cards, reckoning as follows:

Ace	11 each
King	4 each
Queen	3 each
Jack	2 each
Ten	10 each
9, 8, 7	0

An alternative object, if the hand of cards merits the attempt, is to win all eight tricks. This need not be bid or announced beforehand in order to be valid.

Play. Cards rank in their normal order (Ace high, Seven low), with the Ten in its usual place between Nine and Jack – even though it counts 10 points when captured. The player on dealer's left leads to the first trick. Normal rules of trick-taking apply: follow suit if possible; if not, play from any suit. The trick is taken by the highest card of the suit led, and the winner of a trick leads to the next.

Score. At the end of the game each player totals the value of counting cards that he has taken in tricks (as a check, the four totals should make 120 in aggregate). The player with the lowest total scores 5, second lowest 4, third lowest 3, and the player with the most scores 0. In the event of a tie, benefit is given to the 'elder' of the tying players (i.e. the player reached first when counted leftwards from the dealer, dealer himself being 'youngest'). If a player takes all eight tricks, he scores 12 and the others nought.

If the game is played for stakes, as the original was, the dealer puts up 12 units at the start of the game and they are split 5–4–3 as described above. A player who took all eight tricks is paid four units by each opponent, and the pool is carried forward to the next deal, payments from it being doubled.

Hints on play

The interest of Bassadewitz, as opposed to other trick-avoidance games, lies in the score that attaches to individual cards, and especially to the high score of the mid-ranking Ten. This is always a good card to throw to someone else's trick. From the other point of view, if in any suit you lack the Ten but hold higher ranks, you must watch the fall of cards carefully and not lead a face card until the Ten has gone. The Ten is a good card to lead if you hold at least one lower; if you do not, there is a two-to-five chance (as in Slobberhannes) that the three lower cards will fall to it and leave you with the penalty.

When void in a suit, discard the highest-scoring card you can; conversely, lead a low rank when embarking upon a suit for the second or third time round, for fear that a player void in it will force you to capture an Ace or Ten in the trick.

When you have sufficient experience of the game to be able to control your cards well, and the opportunity arises to do so, it is worth keeping track of which player or players have yet to take tricks and attempting to 'reserve' a spare Ace or Ten to throw to them when they start to do so, rather than dropping it at the first available opportunity.

If you must win a trick, play as high as you dare. For example, suppose you hold the Ace and Ten only of a suit, and a lead of the Nine is followed by the Eight and the Seven. Even for the extra point against you, you must take with the Ace (not the Ten), then lead the Ten out: whoever takes it will probably pick up at least 17 to your 11 points. Or again, suppose you hold Ace, Nine, and the player on your right leads the Jack on the first appearance of that suit. Take it with the Ace. Almost certainly the leader will have played from Jack, Ten and nothing lower – he certainly wouldn't lead the Jack if he didn't have the Ten, and if he had any rank lower than the Ten he would have led the Ten rather than the Jack. If now you play the Nine, you leave yourself with an Ace, which will probably be forced later to take the Ten as well for a penalty of at least 21, and possibly an additional 10 or 11 from a player void in the suit, as opposed to the 13 which your early Ace capture entails.

Sample game

South	♠Q 9	♡J T	♣A	♢T 9 8
West	♠A J	♡K	♣J T 7	♢K 7
North	♠8	♡Q 9 8	♣8	♢A Q J
East	♠K T 7	♡A 7	♣K Q 9	♢—

South leads, and his preoccupation lies with the ♣A, which he is unlikely to be able to lose safely.

	S	W	N	E	
W17	♡ T	♡ K	♡ Q	♡ 7	A standard lead, giving West 17 points.
S 21	♣ A	♣ T	♣ 8	♣ 9	An equally standard return, giving his 21.
E 24	♡ J	♠ A	♡ 9	♡ A	West, void in hearts, throws his most dangerous card.
W12	♠ 9	♠ J	♠ 8	♠ T	
E 19	♣ Q	♣ J	◇ A	♣ Q	West has a safe lead, as only the King and Queen remain.
E 7	◇ 9	◇ K	♡ Q	♠ 7	East has no choice, and must take this and the final tricks.
E 6	◇ 8	◇ 7	◇ J	♠ K	South is holding his Ten back, hoping to throw it to
E 14	◇ T	♣ 7	♡ 8	♣ K	North, who has taken none.

120 = 21 + 29 + 0 + 70	*for points taken in tricks*
4 3 5 0	*score*

Gambling games usually work best with a minimum of five players, but for the sociable number four probably the most successful is Pontoon, a round game of the banking variety.

Pontoon is the only name by which I have ever heard the game called in actual play, though all the books call it Vingt-un, which is not-quite-French for the magic number twenty-one on which all the excitement hinges. American writers have stated that the British call it Van John, which I have never heard, and that Pontoon is the Australian name, for which I cannot vouch. The American equivalent is Blackjack – but it is only an equivalent, and far from being the same game. Although the mathematics is much the same, any strategy applicable to one is likely to prove unworkable for the other. In any case, Blackjack is played almost exclusively in casinos – British as well as American – whereas Pontoon is essentially a game of pub and home. And long may it remain so.

The name 'Pontoon' is an intriguing mystery. That it derives from 'punting' strikes me as unlikely because the stress is on the wrong syllable, but the only offer I can propose is a two-stage corruption of Vingt-un. This assumes that it was first pronounced 'vont-oon' by the same First World War dialect of *franglais* that transformed 'billet-doux' into 'billy-do', and then became 'pontoon' under the common process of folk-etymology whereby meaningless words are transformed into their nearest meaningful equivalents (the stock example being 'asparagus' into 'sparrow-grass'). It is well known that Pontoon was the most popular forces' gambling game in both World Wars, circumstances in which real pontoons – flat-bottomed boats useful in the construction of makeshift bridges – would have made the word a commoner element of vocabulary than it is now.

As befits a game of pub, home and World War, there are neither standard rules nor standard terminology. All that can be claimed for the following account is that it is the South London version on which I was brought up.

The game

Cards. A standard 52-card pack.

Preliminaries. Pontoon is played for chips, counters or other manageable objects. Agree first on minimum and maximum permitted stakes (say, one to five), then each player should start with at least ten times the maximum stake (say fifty). Each deal is a separate event and is settled individually. The game ends when one player goes broke, or after an agreed time-limit. Choose first banker by drawing a card from the pack: Ace counts high, and highest banks first. The bankership subsequently passes to the first punter (player against the bank) to make a winning pontoon.

Shuffling. The cards are shuffled before the game starts, and by each player when he takes over the bank. After each deal the banker returns all played cards to the bottom of the pack and cuts, but does not shuffle, before dealing. (Players may agree beforehand to dispense with the cutting rule.)

Value of cards. Cards are only of interest for their numerical values, suit being completely irrelevant. Court cards count ten each, others their face value, and Ace either one or eleven at the discretion of the holder (and he may change his mind about it as often as he likes). Cards worth ten (T J Q K) are called tenths.

Object of the game. At each round of play each punter's object is to acquire a better hand of cards than the banker's. In the event of equality, the banker always wins. The value of a hand is the total value of the cards it comprises. The possible hands rank as follows:

> Bust (over 21) – always loses, but banker wins equality.
> A count of 16 to 21 – the higher, the better.
> Pontoon – a count of 21 consisting of two cards, an Ace and a tenth.

Five-card trick – five cards not exceeding 21 in sum.

Royal pontoon – 21 made on three Sevens (only valid when held by a punter: in the banker's hand it is an ordinary '21').

The deal and stake. The banker deals one card face down to each player, in clockwise rotation ending with himself. Each punter (but not the banker) looks at his card and places a stake beside it, leaving the card face down on the table before him. The banker then deals everyone a second card face down.

Pontoons ? The banker now looks at his cards, without revealing them, to see if he has a pontoon (an Ace and a tenth). If so he shows it, and each punter pays him twice his stake, unless he also has a pontoon, in which case he shows it and only loses his single stake. If the banker does not have a pontoon he leaves his cards face down and indicates his readiness to play further. In this event, any player holding a pontoon must face his Ace to show that he cannot lose and will be taking over the bankership.

Pairs ? Any punter who has two cards of the same rank may split them, and play them as two separate hands. For this purpose they must be of the same rank: different tenths, such as a Queen and a Jack, will not do. The player indicates that he is splitting by separating the two cards, laying the whole of his stake against one of them and placing exactly the same amount as his stake against the other. The banker than deals him two more cards, one for each hand. Again, the punter looks at his second cards, and may split again if he has another pair. In all subsequent play, a punter who has split pairs must count himself as two (or more) separate people, and concern himself with each hand individually.

Stick, buy, twist or bust. The banker now addresses himself to each player in turn, dealing him as many more cards as requested, until the punter either sticks or announces himself bust. So long as the punter's count is less than 16 he must either buy or twist another card. At a count of 16 or more he may buy or twist, or else stick, thus indicating satisfaction with his hand and his intention to compete against the bank. At a count of 22 or more he must announce himself bust and hand his cards to the banker, who returns them to the bottom of the pack and appropriates the loser's stake.

If the punter says 'buy' the banker deals him a card face down; if he says 'twist', the card is dealt face up. In order to buy a card the punter must first increase his stake, but he must not pay less than he did for the previous card, nor more than the total already staked. As soon as he has twisted a card, he may only acquire more by twisting and may not revert to buying. If he gets a total of four cards with a combined count of 11 or less, so that he is bound to make a five-card trick, he may not buy but only twist a fifth. In any case, even when he (legally) buys a fifth card it is dealt face up instead of down. No player may have more than five cards in any one hand.

The banker's play. If everybody busts, the bank wins all stakes and there is no further play. If any punter is left in, however, the banker now reveals his two cards and continues to deal himself more cards, face up, until he either sticks or busts. (He may not split pairs.)

If the banker busts, each punter left in the game reveals his own cards and collects from the banker an amount equivalent to his stake if he has a count of 16 to 21, or twice his stake if he has a pontoon or a five-card trick, or three times his stake if he has a royal pontoon (three Sevens).

If the banker sticks at a count of 21 he wins the single stake of any punter with 21 or less, but is beaten by and pays out a single stake to a punter's pontoon, double stake to a five-card trick, treble stake to a royal pontoon. If his count is less than 21 he pays anyone with a higher count. (With a count of 17, for example, he says 'Pay 18', and anyone with 18 or more turns his cards face up to claim payment.)

If the banker has a five-card trick he beats anything except pontoon and royal pontoon. Banker's royal pontoon (three Sevens) counts only as an ordinary 21, and loses to pontoons and five-card tricks.

See Table for greater clarity.

Bank take-over. The bank is taken over by any punter who wins a pontoon (not a royal pontoon or a five-card trick), but not if he does so on a split hand. If more than one has a pontoon, it goes to the first of them to the present banker's left.

Table of eventualities at Pontoon

Punter's hand	is beaten by banker's:	is paid if unbeaten:
bust (over 21)	anything	—
count of 16–21	equal or higher count	single stake
pontoon (A+tenth)	pontoon only	double stake
five-card trick	five-card trick*	double stake
royal pontoon	—(unbeatable)	treble stake

*Not pontoon, since if the banker had one nobody could have drawn five cards! In some circles, incidentally, a banker's five-card trick beats a pontoon. This marginally increases the excitement on some hands, but it contravenes the spirit of the game, and anything which further increases the banker's advantage (as this does) is to be deprecated.

Hints on play

Skill at gambling consists in playing systematically, though not necessarily to a 'system'; adjusting the amount of your stake to the probability of winning; and resisting the temptation to stake wildly when low on resources. My recommended one-to-five minimum/maximum stake enables you to (a) distinguish between a low, a middling and a high stake, in accordance with the probabilities, and (b) adjust this scale to your current resources. For example, when low on funds you should play cheese-paringly and fix your stakes at, say, 1, 2 or 3; when well off you may fix them at 2, 3, 4 or 3, 4, 5; or at any other time work to a 1, 3, 5 series of gradations.

Do not underestimate the bank's advantage. Most of the banker's income derives from punters who bust, for they still pay him whether or not the banker himself busts. Another large proportion comes from the fact that he wins from equals. And, in his own play, he has an advantage in knowing how many punters are standing against him. As a player, your safest course is to stick when you can – even at 16, since the mean value of a card is seven, and the chances of your not busting are 2–1 against. The banker may conceivably stick at 16 if there is only one punter against him, but with three against him (or up to six, counting split hands) the draw of another card is more likely to win than an agreement to 'pay seventeens'.

The probability that the banker has a pontoon, or that you will be dealt one from scratch, is about 0.024, equivalent to less than $2\frac{1}{2}$ per cent, or one in every 41 hands. (Hence, in a four-player game expect to see a pontoon once in every ten deals.) The probability of being dealt a five-card trick from scratch, according to my calculations, is twice as high – amounting to about 0.045, or $4\frac{1}{2}$ per cent, or one in every 22–23 hands. If fewer actually appear than this figure suggests, it is clearly because many potential five-card tricks are not filled out, but abandoned at the fourth or even third card. The probability that the banker will bust after you have stuck is about 0.3, or three in ten. This figure assumes that he follows the policy of always sticking when he can; if not, your chances improve.

The fact that an Ace may count 1 or 11 introduces some fascinating complications. In Blackjack terminology a hand containing an Ace and not exceeding 21 is described as 'soft'; if it exceeds 21 by counting the Ace as 11 it is 'hard'. It is pretty obvious that you should always stick at, say, 18 – but what about a 'soft' 18, which alternatively counts 8? Here the answer depends in part on how many cards you have – with four, for example, a count of 8 guarantees you a five-card trick; with three, you must consider the possibility of drawing an Eight or Nine, which gives you a lower stickable number, an Ace, Two or Three, which gives you a 21 or a five-card trick, a tenth, which leaves you back where you started (with 18), or one of the other four ranks, which complicate matters further.

Whether or not to split pairs is not a difficult question provided that you follow a policy in deciding which counts are good and which bad. If the individual count of each card is better than the total count of both, split them; otherwise, don't. All you need then is a good policy.

In view of the possibility of a five-card trick, the number of cards on which you reach a given count is of considerable significance. The following suggestions for strategy are therefore subdivided into the numbers of cards held.

First card. Stake high on an Ace, for obvious reasons. The probability of being dealt a tenth next is about 0.38, giving two chances in five of making a pontoon. On a tenth, stake high, but with reservations. The probability of a pontoon is less than 0.08 (12–1 against). You have a three-in-ten chance of getting a second tenth, and must weigh that against the possibility that banker will make 20 or 21. In straitened circumstances, make it a middling stake. On anything else, prefer to stake low.

Second card (no pair). Stick on 16–20 (hard): your chances of *not* busting if you twist at 16 are barely two in five, and naturally worse on higher numbers. The banker will certainly beat your 16 if he sticks, but it is safer to bank on his busting than to try it yourself. On a soft 18–20, stick if you want to play it safe. Soft 16/17 is better counted as 6/7.

A hard count of 12–15 is the worst range of all, and the safest procedure is to twist. The fact that the mean value of a card is seven should not be taken to imply that 14 is the most promising count: 12 is clearly better, as it gives you the smallest chance of busting. A soft count of 12–15 should, of course, be regarded as 2–5.

A count of 10 or 11 is highly favourable – see *First card* for the probabilities. Buy, rather than twist.

On a count of less than 10, buy, for a modest amount. Do not start splashing out yet against the possibility of a five-card trick.

Splitting pairs. Aces: you will do better to split than to regard them as the foundation of a five card trick.

Tenths: the question here is whether a count of 20 in the hand is better than two chances of a pontoon in the bush. It surely is. Don't split.

Nines: your choice is to stick at 18, or to try for two slightly-better-than-even chances of not doing worse. Don't split unless you can afford to indulge a delight in gambling for the sake of it.

Eights: your choice is to stick at 16, twist to a 5-in-13 chance of improving, or split on two 9-in-13 chances of improving a count of eight. Splitting is best; sticking worst.

Sevens, Sixes: neither rank allows you to stick, and both put you in the dreaded 12–15 range. Always split. (The odds of a royal pontoon from a pair of Sevens are 24–1 against.)

Don't split Fives, as 10 is a good count to buy to. Split Fours: it's true that they are of a favourable average value for a five-card trick, but the chances are not good, and 8 is a bad count to buy to. Don't split Threes or Twos: both 6 and 4 are acceptable counts to buy to, and you may be permitted the thought of a five-card trick.

Third card. Stick on hard 16–21. If you must gamble on soft 20, twist, don't buy: you have one chance of improving, four of equalising, eight of doing worse. Whether you count this as only a five-in-thirteen chance of not doing worse, or an eight-in-thirteen chance of not doing better, the odds are still not in your favour. Soft 18 or 19 is best left alone, but you may twist (or even buy, if you can afford it) to soft 16 or 17, either of which is at least in the running for a five-card trick.

With 12–15 (hard), twist, as for the same total on two cards. Count soft 14–15 as 4–5 and buy with a view to a five-card trick. If you have soft 13, you have been playing it all wrong, and soft 12 on three cards is only obtainable with a card counting zero, which Pontoon has not yet invented.

Buy gladly with 10 or 11, and with a view to a five-card trick on a count of 4-7. Buy cheaply or twist, on a count of 8-9.

Fouth card. If you have from 5 to 11, you are obliged to twist, as the five-card trick is beyond question. From 12 to 20, of course, your only concern is not to bust, and the probability of doing so gradually increases as follows:

Count of 12 : 0.31 *probability* (3 *in* 10 *chances of busting*)
        13 : 0.38
        14 : 0.46
        15 : 0.54

16 : 0.62
17 : 0.69
18 : 0.77
19 : 0.85
20 : 0.92

In general, then, you may consider buying so long as your chances of not busting are better than even, i.e. up to a count of 14. You can't stick at 15, so whether you buy or twist is a question that must be answered by balancing the slightly-worse-than-even chance of improving against how much you can afford to gamble.

From 16 upwards the probability of making a five-card trick is exactly the same as that of improving a similar count on a smaller number of cards. However, the difference is that you now stand to win twice your stake if successful as against losing only your single stake if you bust. At 16, then, you have 62 chances in 100 of losing one stake (*total:* minus 62), but 38 chances of gaining two stakes (*total:* plus 76). This produces a balance of +8 in your favour, so at 16 it is worth buying if you can afford it, or twisting if not. At a count of 17, a similar calculation of the balance turns out to be almost the same amount against you, so it would be slightly better to stick. At 18 or more, you should stick.

Banker's play. The same suggestions as those made above for punters apply also when you are the banker, only more so, since you have a natural advantage. If you always stick when you can, you are bound to win in the long run. But, since you don't know how long a run you are going to get, you may be influenced in some of your decisions by the number of punters standing against you. For example, with three against you it is hardly worth sticking at 16; with only one against you, you will already have gained two stakes and can well afford to take another card to a count of 16.

Sample round

The players are Abel, Baker, Charlie and Dealer (banker), who distributes cards as follows:

First two cards

A is dealt ♣3, stakes 3, dealt ♣2 for a count of 5.
B is dealt ♡K, stakes 4, dealt ♠2 for a count of 12.
C is dealt ♡8, stakes 2, dealt ♠8, splits, staking 2 on each count of 8.
C-right is dealt ♢6, counts 14.
C-left is dealt ♠3, counts 11.
D deals himself ♠A ♢2, counts 3 or 13.

Further transactions

A (staking 3 on 5) buys ♣T for 2, counts 15
(staking 5 on 15) twists ♡5, sticks at 20.
B (staking 4 on 12) twists ♣9, sticks at 21.
C-right (staking 2 on 14) twists ♠K, busts.
C-left (staking 2 on 11) buys ♡A for 2, counts 12
(now staking 4 on 13) twists ♢A, counts 14, twists ♣4 for 18 on a five-card trick.
Dealer is now facing three hands (out of four) on a count of 3 or 13. Draws ♠Q for 13, ♡7 for 20, announces 'Pay twenty-ones'.

Result

Abel (20) pays 5 to Dealer ...	−5 for A
Baker (21) receives 4 from Dealer ...	+4 for B
Charlie Right (bust) pays 2 to Dealer ...	+6 for C
Charlie Left (five cards) receives 2 × 4 from Dealer ...	
	−5 for D

Variants

Gambling games vary more widely and change faster than any other type of game, which is why book descriptions of Vingt-un tend to sound archaic (it should be regarded as a forerunner of Pontoon rather than the same game).

In some circles, a pontoon is strictly defined as an Ace and a 'royal', Ace and Ten being only an ordinary 21. The objection to this is that it increases the banker's advantage by reducing a punter's chance to take over by 25 per cent.

Some permit the banker to look at his first card before dealing out any seconds, and, if he likes what he sees, to announce 'Double'. In this case all players must double the stake they have placed on their first card before the seconds are dealt. Again, it may be objected that this works to the banker's advantage.

There are various ways of changing the bankership. The least satisfactory, though clearly the fairest, is for each player to deal in turn. Or the banker may offer to sell the bankership, or entertain an offer to buy it, at any time, so long as the price is acceptable. This is usually followed when the banker has been playing so badly that he cannot afford to lose too heavily on the following round.

A Joker may be conveniently put to use as a marker card. Place it at the bottom of the pack before the first deal. When it appears at the top, shuffle the cards, or allow the bankership to pass to the left or be sold by auction.

GLOSSARY OF TERMS

(Omitted from this list are terms that apply to specific games and are adequately introduced in the appropriate chapters.)

Adverse. Belonging to, or associated with, one's opponents.

Auction. Period after the deal but before the play, when players bid for the right to determine the circumstances of the game.

Balanced hand. One in which the suits are fairly evenly distributed. In Whist, for example, a 4-3-3-3 distribution is balanced, 6-3-3-1 unbalanced.

Bid. Offer to beat other players and achieve a guaranteed score in return for the right to specify conditions of play (e.g. a trump suit).

Biddable suit. One in which you hold sufficient strength to justify nominating it as trumps.

Blue Peter. In Whist, playing (apparently unnecessarily) a higher-ranking card before a lower in order to ask your partner to lead trumps. A similar device, not strictly designated by the term, is the playing of the higher before the lower of a suit in which you hold two cards only, to show that you have voided it after the play of the second.

Combination. A group of cards related by rank or suit or both, and valid for scoring by the particular rules of the game concerned. For Poker combinations, see chapter or summary on Concerto.

Command. The highest card of a suit left in play – for example, the Queen after the Ace and King have been played (in Whist). The player holding such a card is said to have command of the suit.

Contract. An understanding to beat the other players and achieve a guaranteed minimum score in return for the right to specify conditions of play. That which the 'highest bid' becomes when the other players have passed.

Convention. A stroke of play made primarily for the purpose of conveying information to one's partner in accordance with a prearranged coding system; or, the system itself. Whist and Concerto feature conventional leads (the choice of card played gives information about the rest of the hand); Contract Whist also features conventional bids.

Count. The combined numerical value of a hand of cards, determined according to whatever system is in use for the particular game. (Used in Pontoon, and for determining the strength of a hand for bidding purposes, as in Contract Whist.)

Counter. A card which in itself has a scoring value credited to the player who wins it in a trick.

Court cards. King, Queen, Jack.

Cross-ruff. Denotes the play that ensues when each of two partners has a void in a different suit, and each in turn leads a card of his partner's void, enabling him to trump (ruff) and lead back into the other void.

Cut-throat. Describes a game in which each person plays for himself and no partnership play occurs (in an honest game). See *Solo.*

Deadwood. In a Rummy game, cards left in hand, unmelded, when the game ends.

Defender(s). The opponent(s) of the player(s) who made the contract (in defiance of common sense, which demands that the contract should be described as being defended by whoever made it).

Discard. Generally, to play a card from the hand other than for the purpose of winning a trick or making a score. In trick-taking games, a player who has no card of the suit led discards by playing a card from any other suit except trumps. In Rummy games, a player discards by playing a card useless to himself onto the discard pile.

Distribution. The relative number of cards of each suit in a single player's hand, or, generally, the way in which all the suits are distributed amongst the hands of all the players.

Double. Offer to double the score of the game about to be played, made by a player who thinks he (or his partnership) can beat the contract made by his opponent(s).

Doubleton. The holding of exactly two cards of a given suit.

Eldest. The player on the dealer's left, who usually makes the first move.

Establish. In Whist particularly, and trick-games generally, to force out adverse high cards from a given suit so that one can retain permanent command of it.

Face. A face card is a card with a face on it (King, Queen, Jack). A *faced* card is one lying face up, whether there is a face on it or not.

Finesse. In trick games, to attempt to win a trick with a card that is not the highest of its suit left in play.

Follow (suit). Play a card of the same suit as the one that was led to the trick.

Force. In Whist etc., to lead a suit in which another player is void in order to compel him to trump or lose the trick. In Contract Whist, a conventional bid which demands that one's partner should not pass.

Fourth best. The fourth highest card of a suit in one's own hand. The lead of one's fourth best in Whist games conveys useful information to a partner, enabling him to employ the *rule of eleven* (qv).

Game. This word has various shades of meaning according to the context. (*i*) A previously agreed number of deals or rounds may be said to constitute a game, which is won by the player with the highest aggregate score at the end of them. (*ii*) It may mean the previously agreed total of points which, when achieved by any player, ends the game, regardless of the number of rounds or deals taken to reach it. (*iii*) It may mean the conditions of play of a particular deal, as specified by the contractor or highest bidder. In Solo Whist, for example, 'solo in hearts' is a different game from 'solo in clubs' or 'abondance in hearts'.

Guard. A lower card which prevents a higher one from being captured when a still higher card is played to the trick. A King, for example, needs one guard to prevent its capture by the Ace; a Queen requires two to prevent its capture by the Ace or King. (See chapter on Whist)

Hand. The cards held by one player. Also, the player himself.

High. Describes highest card of a particular suit left in play; the card in command of a suit at any given point.

Honours. The significant high cards. In Whist, for example, the Ace, King, Queen, Jack and Ten of a suit.

Lead. To play the first card to a trick. One is said to *lead up to* the person who plays last to the trick, usually the player on one's right, and to *lead through* any other player, including (usually) one's partner.

Long. Describes a suit in which one has more than the average number of cards. For example, if 52 cards are divided between four players, each receives an average of $3\frac{1}{4}$ cards in each suit. A holding of four in the suit is therefore 'long'. In Whist, a long card is one that will win a trick unless trumped.

Meld. A scoring combination of cards laid face up on the table. (Rummy and Canasta.) To meld is to make such a combination and lay it out.

Misère. The deliberate winning of no tricks, or an attempt or contract to win none.

Odd trick. Any trick in excess of half the total number available, or (at Whist) specifically one's seventh won trick (out of thirteen). Not the same as *over-trick*.

Overbid, overcall. To make a higher bid than the preceding one.

Over-trick. Any trick taken in excess of the number bid or contracted.

Partnership. Two or more players who play cooperatively and score the same amount if they win. A four-player partnership game usually implies two-against-two, with predetermined partnerships. In a solo game, three players combine to defeat the contract of the soloist.

Pass. To refrain from making a bid.

Plain suit. In a trump game, any suit other than trumps.

Rank. The order of cards within a suit, e.g. A K Q J T 9 8 7 6 5 4 3 2, or the denomination of each one, e.g. Ace is the highest rank, Two the lowest. May also denote the relative order of suits, e.g. for bidding purposes.

Renounce. Fail to follow suit to the card led because void in that suit. (Strictly speaking, to discard instead of playing a trump in that situation.)

Revoke. Fail to follow suit to the card led, even though not void in the suit and required to follow by the rules of the game. An irregularity for which a penalty is usually exacted.

Round. Constituent part of a game; same as a deal. Also, the playing out of a trick, as in 'after three rounds of clubs, trumps were led'.

Rubber. In Whist, two games won by the same partnership. The first to win two games wins the rubber, which therefore consists of two or three games as may be necessary.

Ruff. To play a trump when void of the suit led.

Rule of eleven. If a player leads the fourth best of his holding in a given suit, the numerical rank of that card when subtracted from eleven shows how many higher cards are against him (i.e. not held by him). For its significance in Whist games, see page 14.

Short suit. Opposite of *long suit*, (qv).

Side-suit. Same as *plain suit*, (qv).

Singleton. The holding of only one card in a given suit.

Soft (Pontoon). A hand containing an Ace that may be counted as 11 without busting. (The term is borrowed from Blackjack.)

Trick. The contribution of one card by each player. The four cards constitute a trick, which is won by the person playing the best card to it.

Trump. One of the suits nominated as best by the rules of the game or the player making the highest bid, such that any card of that suit beats any card of any other (plain) suit regardless of rank. To play a trump.

Turn-up. A card turned up at the start of a game (e.g. to determine the trump suit, or to start the discard pile).

Under-trick. A trick less than the number contracted. Thus a player bidding nine but taking only seven is penalised for two under-tricks.

Void. Holding no cards of any given suit.

Wild card. One that has no independent value but may be counted as part of the meld to which it is added (Rummy, Canasta).

GAME SUMMARIES

Whist (*pp. 3–29*)

52 cards, deal 13 each in ones.
Lead by eldest hand. Usual rules of trick-taking.

Score. Rubber is best of two games. Game is 5 points.

Per odd trick	1 pt	not scorable by partnership standing at 4 to game.
Three honours	2 pts	
Four honours	4 pts	

Conventional leads. Following R. F. Foster's simplified system:

Plain suit

From A K ... or K Q ...	lead K (unless holding K Q J)
From A Q ... or A J ...	lead A
From Q J T ...	lead Q
From K Q J ...	lead J
From K J T ...	lead T

From any other, lead fourth best
From three-card suit, lead highest

Trump suit

From A K Q J T ...	lead J then Q
From A K Q ...	lead Q then K
From A K and 5+ cards	lead K then A
From A K and 4— cards	lead fourth best

Rule of eleven. If fourth best is led, deduct its numerical value from eleven to discover number of higher cards lacking from leader's hand. If led by partner, further deduct number of higher cards in own hand to discover how many held between opponents.

Contract Whist (*pp. 30–52*)

52 cards, deal 13 each in ones.
Lead by player left of declarer. Usual rules of trick-taking apply.

Score. Rubber is best of two games. Game is won by first to reach score of 10 below the line. Figures in parentheses denote score if doubled or re-doubled.

Per odd trick contracted at NT	4	(8)	(16)	below the line
Per odd trick contracted in suit	3	(6)	(12)	below
Per over-trick whether NT or suit	2	(5)	(10)	above
Bonus for winning doubled contract	—	(5)	(10)	above
If lost, opponents score per under-trick		10	(20) (40)	above
Bonus for winning the rubber	50			

Bidding. Low to high: ♣ ◇ ♡ ♠ NT.
Point count strength assessment: Ace 4, King 3, Queen 2, Jack 1.
Distribution assessment: Void 3, Singleton 2, Doubleton 1.
   Usual meaning and interpretation of opening bids:

1 *in suit:* Shows 13+ and longest suit, or higher-ranking of two equally long. Promises re-bid if partner responds showing best suit.

1 *no trump :* Shows 16+ and balanced distribution. Promises 1 NT if partner passes, but invites suit nomination.

2 *in suit:* Shows 24+, demands partner bid his best suit, promises rebid.

2 *no-trump:* Shows balanced hand of 21+. Promises 2 NT if partner passes, but invites nomination of good suit.

3 *in suit:* At least seven held in suit named, but useless for any other bid. Partner passes if weak, bids 3 NT to show general support, or names own suit if holding a strong imbalance.

3 *no-trump:* Shows 23+, safety in all suits and probably nine tricks without assistance. Partner passes, raises to 4 NT or bids strong suit.

4 *in suit:* At least seven cards held in suit shown, and probably eight tricks without partner's support. Partner should keep bidding if possible.

Euchre (*pp. 53–64*)

32 cards (4×A K Q J T 9 8 7). Deal five each (3+2 or 2+3).
Turn next card for prospective trump – dealer may take it if accepted. Bid to accept trump. If all pass, bid to name own suit.
Maker may elect to play alone. If so, either opponent may play alone.
Lead by eldest, or else by player on left of solo maker.
Usual rules of trick-taking apply.

Rank of cards

>   Right bower (Jack of trumps)
>   Left bower (other Jack of same colour)
>   Ace
>   King
>   Queen
>   Jack (except in trumps and matching colour)
>   Ten, Nine, Eight, Seven.

Score. Game is 5 points.

Making side wins three or four tricks	1 point
Making side wins march (5) partnership	2 points
Making side wins march (5) solo	4 points
Making side euchred, opponents score	2 points
If solo opponent euchres maker	4 points

Klaverjass (*pp. 65–75*)

32 cards (4×A K Q J T 9 8 7). Deal eight each in batches of four, and turn up a card to show prospective trump.
Bid for own partnership to take a majority of points in play using turned up trump. If all pass, bid again in own preferred suit.
Lead made by eldest hand. Usual rules of trick-taking apply, except that if void one *must* trump, and trumps must always be overtrumped if possible.

Rank and value. Rank of cards for trick-taking purposes and scoring value when captured in tricks:

Jass   20 (J of trumps)
Menel   14 (9 of trumps)
Ace   11
Ten   10
King   4
Queen   3
Jack   2 (except in trumps)
Nine   0 (except in trumps)
Eight   0
Seven   0
+10 for winning last trick
=162 trick points in all

Scoring combinations. May be declared from the hand when playing to the first trick, or made on the table as result of cards played to trick, scored by winner of trick:

Four Jacks	200	
Four A, K or Q	100	
Sequence of 5+	100	cards rank A K Q J T 9 8 7 for
Sequence of 4	50	purposes of sequence
Sequence of 3	20	
Marriage (K+Q)	20 (only valid in trump suit)	

Score. If challengers win, they score what they make.
If opponents win, they score own total plus challengers' total.
Game is 1500 points.

Quinto (*pp. 76–84*)

53 cards including Joker. Deal 12 each in ones, last five face down (the 'cachette').
Lead by eldest hand. Usual rules of trick-taking apply.

Score. Rubber is best of two games, winners score rubber bonus of 100. Game is 250 points, made for tricks and quints.

Trumps. Hierarchic trump order, from low to high: ♠ ♣ ◇ ♡.
(Any suit trumps spades, hearts trumps any suit.)

Quints. Scored as and when captured in tricks. Quints are A+4 or 3+2 of a suit, any Five, and the Joker (Quint Royal). Value depends on suit:

Quint Royal 25
Quint in ♡ 20
Quint in ◇ 15
Quint in ♣ 10
Quint in ♠ 5

Tricks. Scored at end of deal, and only if neither side reaches 250 by scoring for quints: 5 each undoubled, 10 doubled, 20 re-doubled.

Cachette. Taken by winner of last trick: scores as trick and for any quints contained.

Joker. Has no trick-taking value, and may be played at any time.

Canasta (*pp. 85–97*)

108 cards (two 52-card packs plus four Jokers). Deal eleven each in ones. Form stock and upcard. Cover upcard if wild or red Three. Game is 5000 points.

At each turn. Draw, meld or lay off, discard. Instead of drawing, take (unfrozen) pack if upcard can be melded or laid off. Frozen pack may only be taken if upcard can immediately be melded with two natural cards from own hand.

Melds. Meld at least three, of which at least two natural and not more than three wild. Natural canasta is seven of the same rank, none wild; mixed canasta is seven including at least four natural cards. A side may not go out until it has melded or built up at least one canasta.

Minimum requirements for initial meld

With a minus score:	15	With under 3000:	90
With under 1500:	50	With 3000+:	120

Value and power of cards. Values count plus in melds, minus in hand.

Jokers	50	Meldable but wild. Freeze pack.
Twos	20	Meldable but wild. Freeze pack
Aces	20	Meldable
High (K–8)	10	Meldable
Low (7–4)	5	Meldable
Black Threes	5	Meldable when going out. Freeze pack to left opponent.
Red Threes	100	each, doubled if all four held. May not be melded or discarded, but revealed when taken. Count plus if side has melded, minus if not. Any in hand undeclared counts minus 500.

Bonuses

For going out	100
For going out blind	200 (instead)
Per natural canasta	500 ⎫ in addition to constituent cards.
Per mixed canasta	300 ⎭

Calypso (*pp. 98–108*)

208 cards (four 52-card packs), shuffled together. Four deals; deal 13 each in ones. Players have personal trumps as shown in diagram. Deal rotates; lead by player on dealer's left.

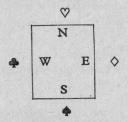

Diagram shows partnerships and personal trumps.

Tricks: plain suit lead. Follow suit if possible; if not possible, win by playing personal trump or lose by discarding. Trick won by highest card of suit led, or highest personal trump if any played, or first-played if equal. (One cannot 'trump' another player's lead of one's own personal trump.)

Tricks: personal trump led. Trick won by leader regardless of rank, unless any players unable to follow play own personal trump, in which case trick won by highest-ranking personal trump, or earliest played if equal.

Score

For first completed calypso	500
For second completed calypso	750
For third (and fourth)	1000 each
For cards in incomplete calypso	20 each
For cards in pile of captures	10 each

Concerto (*pp. 109–123*)

52 cards, deal 13 each in ones. Lead by player left of dealer. Each partnership plays in turn, completing one hand at a time. Lead passes in rotation. Lead may not be passed, but thereafter up to two consecutive passes are permitted between partners. Four Poker hands made, leaving six cards.

Score: Game consists of four deals. Each deal scores as follows:

For combinations: *aggregate value of combinations made*
For opponents' penalty: *five times value of combination left in hand*
For game: 10 points

The 10 for game goes to the side scoring more for combinations, or, if equal, for penalty-bonus.

Penalty. Only five of the six unplayed cards count, but three pairs count 30 to opponents.

Combination	Score	Definition	Type of signal*
Straight flush	15	five in suit and sequence	same suit, same range
Four of a kind	12	four of one rank, one odd	same rank, red then major suit
Full house	8	three-kind and a pair	different rank/suit, three first
Straight	7	in sequence but not suit	not signalled – try straight flush
Flush	6	in suit but not sequence	not signalled – try straight flush
Three of a kind	3	three of a rank, two odd	red 'from threes' and pass
Two pair	2	two pairs, one odd card	black (from pair) and pass
One pair	1	two of a rank, three odd	black (from pair) and pass

*See page 116 for signals in detail.

Solo Whist (*pp. 127–150*)

52 cards. Deal 13 each in threes and one. Turn last card to show preferred trump. Lead by eldest hand, except in a declared abondance, when made by declarer. Usual rules of trick-taking apply. A player who has passed may not re-enter the bidding, except that eldest may accept a proposal despite his previous pass.

Name of bid	Value	Meaning
Proposal and acceptance *Prop and cop*	2	Partners take 8 tricks with preferred trump
Solo	2	Caller takes 5 tricks with preferred trump
Misère	3	Caller takes 0 tricks at no trump
Abondance *Abundance*	4	Caller takes 9 tricks with own trump
Abondance royale *Royal abundance*	4	Caller takes 9 tricks with preferred trump (overcalls a simple abondance)
Misère ouverte *Open or spread misère*	6	Caller takes 0 tricks, with cards exposed (after the first card has been led)
Abondance declarée *Declared abundance*	8	Caller takes 13 tricks at no trump (some players permit own trump)

Auction Pitch (*pp. 151–160*)

52 cards, deal six each in threes.
Pass or bid 1, 2, 3 or 4.
Highest bidder 'pitches' by leading from suit selected by himself as trump.

Tricks. Players are free to follow suit or trump as they prefer, but may only discard if unable to do either.

Points. These features are worth one point each:

High = *Playing the highest trump of the deal*
Low = *capturing in a trick the lowest trump of the deal*
Jack = *capturing the Jack of trumps if in play*
Game = *capturing in tricks the highest aggregate value of cards reckoned as follows:*

Ace	4 each
King	3 each
Queen	2 each
Jack	1 each
Ten	10 each
Others	0

If two players tie, there is no point for game.

Score. If pitcher makes at least the number he bid, he scores the amount he bid (nothing for extra points); if not, he subtracts his bid. Other players score any point they may make. Game is 7 points. To prevent ties, points are scored strictly in order *high, low, jack, game,* and the first to reach the target wins.

Seven Card Rummy (*pp. 161–172*)

52 cards. Deal seven each in ones. Form a stock and face an upcard to start the discard pile.

Object. To meld sequences of three or more in suit (Ace low unless otherwise agreed) or three or four of the same rank. First to meld all cards from hand ends the game; others score penalties for cards left in hand.

Method. Draw face-down card from stock or face-up card from discards, make any melds possible and wished, discard from hand. Individual cards may be melded by being 'laid off' against existing melds, either one's own or opponents'.

Score. Player who goes out scores face value of all cards remaining in opponents' hands (Ace 1, court cards 10 each). For 'going rummy' (melding all seven cards from hand at once) score double. If Ace allowed high, it counts 11.

Reverse Games (*pp. 173–187*)

DOMINO HEARTS

52 cards. Deal six each in ones and form a stock. Eldest leads. Object is to avoid taking hearts. Follow suit if possible; if not, draw from stock until able. After stock exhausted, continue play with usual rules for no-trump games, discarding if unable to follow suit. Score a penalty point for each heart captured in tricks.

SLOBBERHANNES

32 cards (4 × A K Q J T 9 8 7). Cut the pack: highest card leads, and cards are dealt by the player on his right. Follow usual rules of trick play at no-trump.

Penalties: 1 for winning first trick, 1 for winning last trick, 1 for capturing ♣Q, 4 for incurring all penalties (instead of 3).

BASSADEWITZ

32 cards (4 × A K Q J T 9 8 7). Deal eight each in pairs. Eldest hand leads. Follow usual rules of trick play at no-trump.

Object. To take the *lowest* aggregate value of scoring cards in tricks, reckoning as follows:

Ace	11
King	4
Queen	3
Jack	2
Ten	10
Others	0

Total: 30 per suit, *120* in whole pack.

Score. 5 for taking the fewest, 4 for next fewest, 3 for next, 0 for most. If two players tie, the score goes to the elder of them (first one round from dealer's left).
Special score. For taking all eight tricks: 12 (opponents score 0).

Pontoon (*pp. 188–198*)

52 cards.

Deal one each face down. Place stakes (except banker).

Deal second face down.

Banker's pontoon collects double (single from other pontoon holder).

Punter's pontoon declared.

Pairs may be split; same stake on each.

Buy or twist. Stand at not less than 16. Bust at over 21.

Buy not less than previous buy or more than total stake.

Having twisted, may not buy.

Results

Hand	Beaten by banker's	Wins if unbeaten
bust	anything	—
16–21	equal or higher count	1 × stake
pontoon	pontoon	2 × stake
five-card trick	five-card trick	2 × stake
royal pontoon	(unbeatable)	3 × stake

Introducing the World's Most Respected
View on Games

Quite simply, *Games & Puzzles* magazine is unique. There is no other publication quite like it anywhere in the world.

Started four years ago by a small team of games experts, games inventors and journalists who were games devotees, *Games & Puzzles* has since grown substantially to become recognized throughout the world as the leading authority on games, games inventions and games playing.

The magazine is witty, entertaining, and most of all objective and highly informed. So if you're interested in playing, inventing or even making games, it's the one publication in the world you really can't afford to miss.

Special Introductory Offer

For new subscribers we offer a 3-months' trial period so you can vouch for yourself that our magazine really is all we claim. If, during the initial 3-month period, you wish to cancel your subscription, we will immediately refund you your money in full. Please write enclosing your subscription (cheque/money order/postal order) to:

Circulation Manager
Games & Puzzles
11 Tottenham Court Road
London W1A 4XF

Subscription rates:

	One Year	Three Years
United Kingdom	£4·80	£14·40
USA/Canada	$12·00	$36·00
Other Countries	£5·40	£16·20

TEACH YOURSELF BOOKS

CARD GAMES FOR ONE
George F. Hervey

No better amusement has been devised than that of patience, and this book introduces the reader to eighty-seven different patiences, providing an almost inexhaustible supply of new games to play.

Both single and double pack games are to be found here, from the well known Demon, Sir Tommy and Miss Milligan to eight newly devised games which appear in print for the first time. The rules to each game are carefully described and layouts are illustrated wherever helpful.

No patience player is properly equipped without this unique collection of card games.

UNITED KINGDOM	75p
AUSTRALIA	$2.45*
NEW ZEALAND	$2.40
CANADA	$2.50

ISBN 0 340 05538 3   *recommended but not obligatory

TEACH YOURSELF BOOKS

CARD GAMES FOR TWO
Kenneth Konstam

Scores of card games for two have been invented but many are so simple as not to need explanation. The hope of this book is to cover those most commonly-played games for two which are different enough to require complete rules and which, to be played successfully, demand insight into the workings of the game. With the aid of diagrams, nine games in all are described and analysed. The result is a book which will both encourage the player to improve his skill in those he already knows and introduce him to new games which he will find equally fascinating.

UNITED KINGDOM	75p
AUSTRALIA	$2.45*
NEW ZEALAND	$2.40
CANADA	$2.50

ISBN 0 340 05539 1   *recommended but not obligatory

TEACH YOURSELF BOOKS

CARD GAMES FOR THREE
David Parlett

Playing cards is an entertaining and absorbing way to pass any evening and this collection of 3-hand games is ideal for the family as well as for serious card players who lack a fourth for Bridge.

This selection includes the best 3-hand card games from all around the world; Pinochle from America, Skat from Germany, Five Hundred from Australia, Zwikken from Holland, Tyzicha from Russia, Calabrasella from Italy, Ombre from Spain, and in every case the rules and questions of strategy are illustrated by sample games.

This is a book for both beginners and experts. The basic principles of card play are explained and some of the games are elementary, but several rival even Bridge in depth.

UNITED KINGDOM	**£1.50**
AUSTRALIA	**$4.90***
NEW ZEALAND	**$4.70**
CANADA	**$4.95**

ISBN 0 340 21519 4   *recommended but not obligatory

TEACH YOURSELF BOOKS

All these books are available at your local bookshop or newsagent, or can be ordered direct from the publisher. Just tick the titles you want and fill in the form below.
Prices and availability subject to change without notice.

··

TEACH YOURSELF BOOKS, P.O. Box 11, Falmouth, Cornwall

Please send cheque or postal order, and allow the following for postage and packing:

U.K. – One book 22p plus 10p per copy for each additional book ordered, up to a maximum of 82p.

B.F.P.O. and EIRE – 22p for the first book plus 10p per copy for the next 6 books, thereafter 4p per book.

OTHER OVERSEAS CUSTOMERS – 30p for the first book and 10p per copy for each additional book.

Name..

Address..

··